BASIC STUDENT DISCIPLESHIP

Seth Buckley, Randy Fields, Tan Flippin
Kristin Gaddis, & Kevin Hall

LifeWay Press®
Nashville, Tennessee

© 2002 LifeWay Press®
Reprinted 2004, 2005, May 2006

ISBN 0-6330-7370-9

This book is a resource in the Personal Life
category of the Christian Growth Study Plan.
Course CG-0804

Dewey Decimal Classification Number: 248.83
Subject Heading: DISCIPLESHIP TRAINING—YOUTH
CHRISTIAN LIFE

Printed in the United States of America.

Student Ministry Publishing
LifeWay Christian Resources
of the Southern Baptist Convention
One LifeWay Plaza
Nashville, TN 37234-0174

We believe the Bible has God for its author; salvation for its end; and truth,
without any mixture of error, for its matter and that all Scripture
is totally true and trustworthy. The 2000 statement of
The Baptist Faith and Message is our doctrinal guideline.

Unless otherwise indicated, Scripture quotations are from
the Holy Bible, *New International Version*. Copyright © 1973, 1978, 1984
by International Bible Society.

To order additional copies of this resource:
WRITE LifeWay Church Resources Customer Service,
One LifeWay Plaza, Nashville, TN 37234-0113;
FAX order to (615) 251-5933; PHONE 1-800-458-2772;
E-MAIL to *CustomerService@lifeway.com;* ONLINE at *www.lifeway.com;*
or visit the LifeWay Christian Store serving you.

Cover Photography: Photonica/CSA Archive
Text Photography: Photonica/CSA Archive and PhotoDisc

Contents

Getting Started

You are about to begin a great journey. When you came to Christ, your eternal destiny changed. Once you were bound for eternal separation from God in hell. When you placed your faith in Christ, He became your Savior. His Holy Spirit came into your life to seal your salvation. You are now destined to spend eternity with Christ in heaven.

This book begins with the assumption that you know Jesus as your Savior and that you acknowledge Him to be Lord of your life. It is possible that some would pick up this study having never placed their trust in the Lord Jesus Christ. If you have not accepted Him as your Savior and Lord, now is a good time to do so. Ask God to speak to you as you read the following Scriptures.

Romans 3:23	All have sinned.
Romans 6:23	Eternal life is a free gift of God.
Romans 5:8	Jesus loved us and paid our sin debt.
Romans 10:9-10	Confess Jesus as Lord and believe God raised Him from the dead.
Romans 10:13	Ask God to save you and He will.

You probably will have questions; find a pastor, your youth leader, or a Christian friend and discuss your questions with them. Then, pray a prayer like this: *Lord Jesus, I know that I have sinned. Please forgive me of my sins, come into my life and take control. I offer myself to You, so that I can spend eternity with You. In Jesus name, Amen.*

Be sure to let your pastor, Christian friend, or leader know about your decision.

Many Christians seem to believe that once they have trusted Christ as their Lord and Savior, there is nothing left to do but wait for heaven. Nothing could be further from the truth. God calls Christians into an incredible life of discipleship. What is a disciple? A disciple is simply someone who walks with Jesus and does the things that Jesus says to do.

Matthew 4 tells of Jesus calling His first disciples, Simon and Andrew. The two brothers were fishermen on the Sea of Galilee. When Jesus came upon them, they were casting their net into the sea. Jesus told them, "Come, follow me, and I will make you fishers of men." That is His call for you today. First, He calls you to follow Him. How do you do that? Read on. Second, He plans for you to invest your life in the life of others ... and He will show you how.

My Discipleship Group

1. Name: _Kayla Hathcote_   Phone: _____
   Address: _____ e-mail: _____
2. Name: _Kelsey Speer_   Phone: _____
   Address: _____ e-mail: _____
3. Name: _Kelly Wogen_   Phone: _____
   Address: _____ e-mail: _____
4. Name: _Sarah Cady_   Phone: _____
   Address: _____ e-mail: _____
5. Name: _Gale Speer_   Phone: _____
   Address: _____ e-mail: _____
6. Name: _Carissa Molden_   Phone: _____
   Address: _____ e-mail: _____
7. Name: _Christy Grau_   Phone: _____
   Address: _____ e-mail: _____
8. Name: _Jamie Hooker_   Phone: _____
   Address: _____ e-mail: _____
9. Name: _Charis Forcey_   Phone: _____
   Address: _____ e-mail: _____
10. Name: _____ Phone: _____
    Address: _____ e-mail: _____
11. Name: _____ Phone: _____
    Address: _____ e-mail: _____
12. Name: _____ Phone: _____
    Address: _____ e-mail: _____
13. Name: _____ Phone: _____
    Address: _____ e-mail: _____
14. Name: _____ Phone: _____
    Address: _____ e-mail: _____
15. Name: _____ Phone: _____
    Address: _____ e-mail: _____

TITLE
THE COST OF DISCIPLESHIP

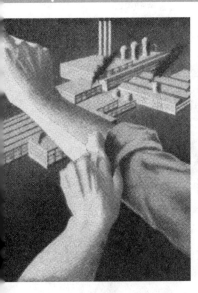
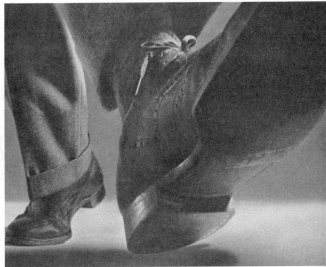

When you became a Christian, you began an incredible journey with Christ. You know the destination: heaven! However, the time between asking Christ to save you and going to heaven is where you may struggle the most. That's what this book is about. As you study through this book with your leader and your discipleship group, you will begin to fill your spiritual tool belt with essential tools for living an effective Christian life. It won't be easy. In fact, it will cost you. However, it is worth the investment. Your life will become more than you ever dreamed it would as you follow Jesus. Let's start with an overview of session 1. (Sessions 2–8 also follow this format.) Each session has seven parts—Group Study, On Your Own, Character Trait Study, Seven-Day Quiet Time Journal, Memory Verse, God-sized Challenge, Week-at-a-Glance Calendar. Each part of this study equips you with spiritual tools to help you live an effective Christian life. Just like a builder needs a hammer for some parts of his job and a saw for others, each of these spiritual tools are necessary for a Christian and important for different parts of your life.

GROUP STUDY

Getting the Most

What kind of car makes you drool? If you went to the car dealer, do you think they would just give you one? Probably not. When things are really valuable, they cost you. The same is true for a real life of discipleship. If you are going to get the most out of this study, it will cost you. What does it cost? Add the missing words to see a few things you will need to do.

1. Bring your _bible_ and this _study book_ with you each week.
2. Make it a _priority_ to _spend time_ with God.
3. Spend time in _quiet time_ every day.
4. _Memorize_ a verse of Scripture each week.
5. Build relationships with others by _listening to them_, and spending time with your _discipleship group_ each week.

You will use the above "tools of discipleship" each week.

What's the Cost?

When Jesus called His disciples He began with a couple of unlikely candidates, fishermen named Simon and Andrew. You can read about their encounter with Jesus in Matthew 4:18-20. Jesus told them, "Come, follow me, and I will make you fishers of men."
They left their boat and followed Him ... just like that.

List below the things you think it cost Simon and Andrew to follow Jesus.

Careers, Family
Friends

Jesus' call to be a disciple is never easy. Read what Jesus said in Matthew 16:24-25. According to these verses, there are three things He expects of a disciple. Write those three "costs of discipleship" in the blanks below.

PHILIPPIANS
3:13-14

1. _Deny Himself_
2. _Take up His Cross_
3. _Follow Me_

Take Up Your Cross

My friend Justin is in high school and is totally devoted to basketball. He loves the game. Practice can be hard; sometimes Justin runs until he feels like his heart will explode. He does drills again and again. Even then, he might not get to play in the game. Most of Justin's friends hang out together after school. Justin misses time with his friends, but he never misses basketball practice. Justin sacrifices a lot to play basketball.

Here's the important question: Are you as committed to following Jesus as Justin is to basketball? Think about it. When Jesus said to "deny yourself," He meant be willing to sacrifice your agenda so that you can do what He wants you to do. In fact, "take up your cross" literally means that Jesus wants His disciples to be willing to die to themselves every day. There may be things that are getting in the way of you being everything God wants you to be. They may not be bad things, but if they are not God's agenda for you, it's time to leave them behind.

PHILIPPIANS 2:1-4

What things in your life do you need to give up in order to follow Jesus?

Did you catch the reason for the self-sacrifice? The idea is for us to be free to follow Jesus. Following Jesus can be a great adventure. Take Rachel for example. She graduated from high school and was headed for a distant college and a high-paying career. However, she sensed that God wanted her to go on a two-week mission trip to Russia the summer after she graduated. While she was on the trip, God did amazing things through her even though she didn't speak Russian. After returning home, she planned to go to a local college to study Russian so she could spend all of next summer doing mission work in Russia. Was she sorry to adjust her agenda? Not when she saw what God had in store for her!

Follow

Following Christ is hard work. You are accountable for your spiritual growth and lifestyle. If you want to know where Jesus is leading you, you will have to invest time in listening. That means being responsible for your personal Bible study, prayer, Scripture memory, and worship. Most of all, it means being obedient to what He tells you—no dragging your feet, belly-aching, or groaning. As you build your relationship with Jesus, little by little, He will prune away things in your life that keep you from Him.

1 PETER 1:14-16

Read John 15:1-2. What do you think it means for God to "prune" your life?

List areas in your life that you need to let God prune away (cut out) so you can grow closer to Him.

ON YOUR OWN

Each week, you will be doing some personal study about the tools discussed in your discipleship group. Don't rush through this study time, but allow God to speak to you as you read and learn.

Following Jesus is going to cost you time. It is not something you get from a sermon, worship service, camp, or discipleship class. You will need a relationship with Jesus. That only happens by spending time with Him.

This week, you are going to start setting aside daily time to spend with Jesus. How do you do that? Here are some simple suggestions. Look up the Scripture references and fill in the blanks.

1 JOHN 5:3

1. **Mark 1:35–Try to spend time with God first thing in the** _morning_.
2. **Matthew 14:23–** _Pray_ **before you read the passage, asking God to speak to you through it.**
3. **Luke 2:52–Look for ways you need to** _change_ **to be more Christlike.**
4. **Luke 2:46–Write any** _questions_ **you have about the passage so you can ask your leader or another Christian later.**

Use the material on the next pages for time alone with God this week. The first box gives you an example to follow. You may discover that you have more questions after reading the Scripture than you have answers for. That's OK! Write down your questions and ask your leader about them later. (Answers for blanks: 1. morning, 2. Pray, 3. grow, 4. questions.)

JOHN 10:10

Each week you will be looking at a character trait you need to develop. When you decide to follow Jesus, regardless of the cost, you will begin to develop the trait of responsibility by putting Him first in your priorities.

CHARACTER TRAIT STUDY

> **Responsibility—** The act of being responsible for oneself and one's actions. In the life of a Christian, it means ultimately being accountable for one's own spiritual growth and lifestyle.

How can you begin to practice this character trait? Is there any evidence of a sense of responsibility in your life right now? If so, in what area?

SAMPLE

☐ PRAY
☐ READ
☐ RESPOND

985003

Pray: (Write out your prayer.) *Dear God, help me this morning as I read Your Word. Help me desire to please You today in all I do. Help me to understand Your Words to me and make them a part of my life.*

Read John 3:30.

What does it mean to allow God to become greater and yourself to become less? *In order for Jesus to be more real to me, there are things in my life that I either need to get rid of or spend less time doing.*

Read John 3:30 again.

What action can you take toward this goal? *I need to quit listening to music that fills my mind with thoughts that are not pleasing to God. Maybe I can get rid of them and replace them with something else that will help.*

Commitment Prayer: (Write out your prayer.) *God, help me to allow the parts of my life that do not please you to decrease so I can be more like You.*

(1) SPEND TIME FIRST THING IN THE MORNING IF AT ALL POSSIBLE, (2) PRAY BEFORE YOU READ THE PASSAGE ASKING GOD TO SPEAK TO YOU THROUGH IT, (3) LOOK FOR WAYS IN YOUR LIFE THAT NEED TO BE CHANGED TO ALLOW YOU TO BE MORE CHRISTLIKE.

SUNDAY

☐ PRAY
☐ READ
☐ RESPOND

985003

Pray:

Read 2 Corinthians 5:17.

Who does this verse say you are now that you are a Christian?

Read 2 Corinthians 5:17 again.

What old ways or habits are you still hanging on to in your new life?

Commitment Prayer:

(1) SPEND TIME FIRST THING IN THE MORNING IF AT ALL POSSIBLE, (2) PRAY BEFORE YOU READ THE PASSAGE ASKING GOD TO SPEAK TO YOU THROUGH IT, (3) LOOK FOR WAYS IN YOUR LIFE THAT NEED TO BE CHANGED TO ALLOW YOU TO BE MORE CHRISTLIKE.

MONDAY

Pray:

☐ PRAY
☐ READ
☐ RESPOND

Read 1 John 5:3.

What does this verse mean that His commands are not burdensome?

985003

Read 1 John 5:3 again.

Are you showing God that you love Him? If yes, how? If no, why not?

Commitment Prayer:

TUESDAY

Pray:

☐ PRAY
☐ READ
☐ RESPOND

Read 1 Peter 1:14-16.

What will you do if you are holy? What will you not do?

985003

Read 1 Peter 1:14-16 again.

In what areas of your life do you need to work on being holy?

Commitment Prayer:

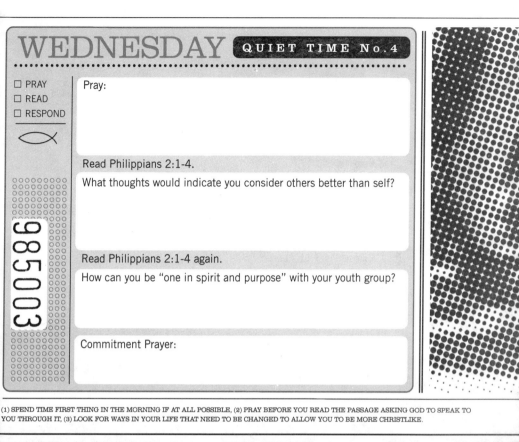

WEDNESDAY

☐ PRAY
☐ READ
☐ RESPOND

985003

Pray:

Read Philippians 2:1-4.

What thoughts would indicate you consider others better than self?

Read Philippians 2:1-4 again.

How can you be "one in spirit and purpose" with your youth group?

Commitment Prayer:

(1) SPEND TIME FIRST THING IN THE MORNING IF AT ALL POSSIBLE, (2) PRAY BEFORE YOU READ THE PASSAGE ASKING GOD TO SPEAK TO YOU THROUGH IT, (3) LOOK FOR WAYS IN YOUR LIFE THAT NEED TO BE CHANGED TO ALLOW YOU TO BE MORE CHRISTLIKE.

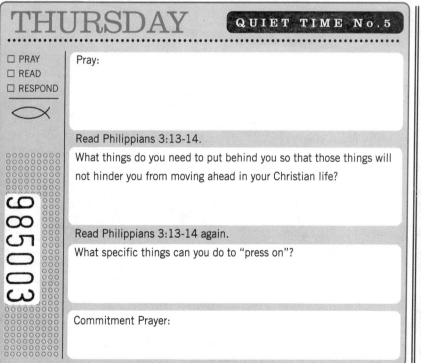

THURSDAY

☐ PRAY
☐ READ
☐ RESPOND

985003

Pray:

Read Philippians 3:13-14.

What things do you need to put behind you so that those things will not hinder you from moving ahead in your Christian life?

Read Philippians 3:13-14 again.

What specific things can you do to "press on"?

Commitment Prayer:

(1) SPEND TIME FIRST THING IN THE MORNING IF AT ALL POSSIBLE, (2) PRAY BEFORE YOU READ THE PASSAGE ASKING GOD TO SPEAK TO YOU THROUGH IT, (3) LOOK FOR WAYS IN YOUR LIFE THAT NEED TO BE CHANGED TO ALLOW YOU TO BE MORE CHRISTLIKE.

FRIDAY

Pray:

☐ PRAY
☐ READ
☐ RESPOND

Read Colossians 3:17.

How do you do something "in the name of the Lord Jesus"?

Read Colossians 3:17 again.

Which is harder for you to do in Jesus' name—word or deed?

Commitment Prayer:

985003

SATURDAY

Pray:

☐ PRAY
☐ READ
☐ RESPOND

Read John 10:10.

How has Satan been like a thief in your life?

Read John 10:10 again.

How have you experienced the full life Jesus brings?

Commitment Prayer:

985003

Do you struggle to memorize Scripture? God really does answer prayer. Ask Him to help you memorize Scripture. Each week you will be given a Bible verse along with a tip you can use to help you memorize it. Use the tip and enlist other people to help you. Make it your goal to memorize the verse each week. Don't give up, you can do it!

MEMORY VERSE FOR THE WEEK

JOHN 3:30

To help you memorize a verse, write it out on a small card. Carry the card with you and read it two or three times a day. You also may wish to write it out several times on a piece of paper. Practice saying it to someone from memory during the week.

God-sized Challenge

Each week you will have a God-sized Challenge. Let's get serious about this challenge! This challenge will help you practice what you have learned in your group and personal study. You will be paired with an accountability partner. Your partner may be your best friend, or you might not know your partner at all. You may be tempted not to follow through with your partner to do a challenge. Remember, this activity is to challenge you to reach beyond yourself to become more Christlike in your thoughts and actions. Don't take a half-hearted approach to discipleship; step up to the God-sized Challenge!

Now it's time to practice what you have learned this week. Team up with your accountability partner, choose one of the God-sized Challenges, and rise to the challenge together. (If you don't have a partner, do a challenge on your own and tell someone how it felt to do something in Jesus' name.)

1. Be a friend this week to someone in your school who is alone most of the time. Sit with them at lunch, invite them to do something with you after school, or ask them to come to your house to study with you. Caution: Keep in mind this person's feelings. Do not simply do this as a one-time activity, but continue treating them like Jesus would so that they will know of your genuine concern and friendship.

2. Do something for an elderly person in your church this week. It may consist of raking leaves in his or her yard, working in his garden, or cleaning her house. If you are not sure who needs to be helped, ask your parents or check with someone in your church office for ideas. Be sure to assist someone who does not have the capability to do these things for himself or herself.

WEEK-AT-A-GLANCE CALENDAR

1. List Your Priorities—These are the things you want to make sure happens this week, such as spending time with God, planning and doing a God-sized Challenge, spending time with your parents, affirming a friend, or confronting someone with a concern.

2. List Essentials—These are the things you have to accomplish this week, such as preparing for tests at school, fulfilling job requirements, home responsibilities, and church activities.

On the following calendar, first write down when you will do your daily quiet time or devotional time each day and when you want to schedule your God-sized Challenge with your accountability partner. Then complete the calendar with other things that you will do this week.

Week-at-a-Glance

Priorities

Essentials

Sunday

MORNING	AFTERNOON	EVENING

Monday

MORNING	AFTERNOON	EVENING

Tuesday

MORNING	AFTERNOON	EVENING

Wednesday

MORNING	AFTERNOON	EVENING

Thursday

MORNING	AFTERNOON	EVENING

Friday

MORNING	AFTERNOON	EVENING

Saturday

MORNING	AFTERNOON	EVENING

TLE **ACCOUNTABLE RELATIONSHIPS** ΙΧΘΥΣ

Your science teacher tells you to read chapter 5. "It's not something we'll spend time on, and it won't be on the test," she says. "In fact, I won't even ask you if you've read it." So the question is ... do you read it? Be honest! You probably won't even crack the book. The truth is, you are most likely to do the things that you know someone will ask you about.

If you are going to do the things that will help you grow as a Christian, you will probably need someone to check on you. An accountability partner is someone committed to you and to your spiritual growth. Their motivation to confront you is always love, but they don't let you off the hook when you fail to do your quiet time or memorize Scripture. Let's take a look at how and why you need to build healthy accountable relationships with other Christians.

GROUP STUDY

The letters that make up the word *team* can also be used to form an acronym to encourage athletes to discover the role teammates play. **What words make up the acronym? Write your answer below.**

T ogether
E veryone
A ccomplishes
M ore

GALATIANS 6:1-5

In 2001, Tom Brady, quarterback for the Super Bowl-winning New England Patriots passed for a total of 2,843 yards. Impressive, huh? However, Steve McNair, quarterback for the Tennessee Titans passed for 3,350 yards, far surpassing Brady. Yet the Titans didn't even make the play-offs. How can this be? A team needs more than a good quarterback to be champions. Even though gifted individuals are on a team, when team members work together, have common goals, and have the same attitude as their coach, the entire team is at its best and wins.

List the teams of which you are a member in the space below.

- Leadership
- Discipleship group

Did you just list sports teams? Do you see your discipleship group as a team? In the teams above, did you list your discipleship group?

PHILIPPIANS 2:3-4

What do you think the quote, *"There are no 'lone-ranger' Christians,"* means?

- we are a TEAM!

One in Heart

Does the fact that we are all Christians mean that we will always work together as a team? Not always. Building relationships in which we are accountable to each other takes effort. Philippians 2:1-5 describes qualities that should characterize relationships between Christians. Without these qualities, there can be no true accountability between believers.

Read Philippians 2:1-5 and complete the blanks below.
1. **Accountable relationships begin with the** love **of** Christ.
2. **Christians must be able to** trust **those who hold them accountable.**
3. **Holding someone accountable means being willing to make** sacrifices

(Answers: love, Christ, v. 1-2; trust, v. 3; sacrifices, v.4.)

- confidentiality
- unconditional love

Developing Accountable Relationships

Let's say that your discipleship group scores a 10 on everything we have talked about so far. You truly love each other in the love of Christ. You can trust each other with anything. You are even willing to make sacrifices for each other. So, what do you do? When you meet with your accountability partner, what is supposed to happen? Every accountable relationship will be as unique as the individuals involved. The longer you have walked together, holding each other accountable, the more personal your relationship will be. Still, here are a few general guidelines for accountability partners.

1. **Pray. (1 Thess. 5:17)** There is absolutely nothing you can do that has more power than prayer. Pray aloud with each other and for each other. It will do your heart good to hear your partner lift you up in prayer. Pray often. When someone says, "Will you pray for me about ...", the right response is, "Yes, let's do that right now."

2. **Be willing to bust the power of secrets. (Jas. 5:16)** Secret sin and secret practices give Satan a lot of power over you. Be honest about your sin and ask your accountability partner to pray for you.

3. **Ask hard questions. (Gal. 3:1-5)** If your partner asks you to pray for his short temper, do. The next day ask him, "How did you do at controlling your temper yesterday?" Then, keep asking him about it. If you know that your partner committed to memorizing a verse a week, ask her how it's going. Don't ask with the motive of catching someone in a fault. Ask because you care enough to ask.

4. **Speak words of encouragement. (Heb. 10:25)** It is easy to feel like a failure. Be a constant source of encouragement to your accountability partner. Don't flatter your partner with lies, but be quick to point out things they do well. Tell your partner at least five things they are doing well for every one thing you suggest they need to work on.

5. **Confront with love and humility. (Gal. 6:1)** If your partner is doing something that you know is sin, you need to confront him. However, begin by searching your own heart. Then ask yourself: Am I really concerned about him? Am I truly wanting her best? Have I put to death my spiritual pride? Then, confront your accountability partner with honesty, but speak every word with love.

Even though you are learning about the above guidelines in relation to accountability partners, these guidelines should be applied to all of our Christian relationships.

Write two specific ways you can put these concepts into practice in your relationships with other Christians.

1. Encourage !

2. Don't gossip !

ON YOUR OWN

Redwood trees, found primarily in California, are in clusters because their root systems are webbed together below the ground to draw strength from one another. This makes them able to grow as high as they do (taller than a football field is long) and to resist weather that might destroy them.

Read Luke 10:1-3. Why do you think Jesus sent the seventy out two-by-two?

Write (or illustrate) an example of how you can experience accountability and the difference it can make on a daily basis. If you choose to illustrate the concept of the difference accountability can make on a daily basis, label your illustration. (For example: Drawing of redwoods labeled "friends," redwood roots webbed together labeled "friends strengthening each other against outside forces," redwood bark labeled "Bible is a believer's shield.")

ACTS
2:42-47

Billy Graham exemplifies responsible awareness, faithfulness, and integrity in a sinful world. Early in his ministry, Graham decided he would remain faithful to his wife and demonstrate integrity in his relationships. He chose never to eat a meal with a woman who wasn't a family member without a third person present. He chose never to let a woman in his hotel room for any reason, even if that person was a coworker. He chose to have aides enter a room first to make certain that no one was already there when he arrived. Other Christian leaders have fallen into sin; but, because of his early decisions, Graham is known for his faithfulness and integrity.[1]

A life of integrity and Christlikeness begins with a plan to guard yourself against anything that would hurt your witness as a Christian. You'll only be successful if you surround yourself with those who share a common goal to be more like Christ.

Begin writing a plan of responsible awareness, faithfulness, and integrity for your life. What do you need to be on your guard about in your Christian walk?

---

1. Rod Handley, *Transparent Living: Living a Life of Integrity* (Nashville: Cross Training Publishing, 1998), 15.

CHARACTER TRAIT STUDY

{ **Faithfulness—** Being steadfast, trustworthy, and truthful. Always seeking to please God. }

One way you can develop faithfulness to God is to know what He wants you to do. Learn what He wants you to do through a daily time alone with Him. Write two ways you can practice this character trait.

1.
2.

Are you a faithful friend? List one way you can be a more faithful friend.

List one way you are faithful in your Christian walk. How could you improve?

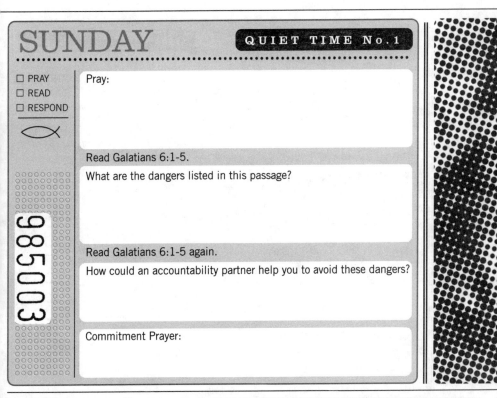

SUNDAY

QUIET TIME No. 1

☐ PRAY
☐ READ
☐ RESPOND

985003

Pray:

Read Galatians 6:1-5.
What are the dangers listed in this passage?

Read Galatians 6:1-5 again.
How could an accountability partner help you to avoid these dangers?

Commitment Prayer:

(1) SPEND TIME FIRST THING IN THE MORNING IF AT ALL POSSIBLE, (2) PRAY BEFORE YOU READ THE PASSAGE ASKING GOD TO SPEAK TO YOU THROUGH IT, (3) LOOK FOR WAYS IN YOUR LIFE THAT NEED TO BE CHANGED TO ALLOW YOU TO BE MORE CHRISTLIKE.

MONDAY

Pray:

☐ PRAY
☐ READ
☐ RESPOND

Read Philippians 2:3-4.

What can you do to help a friend to keep from stumbling?

985003

Read Philippians 2:3-4 again.

Do you struggle with considering yourself better than others?

Commitment Prayer:

(1) SPEND TIME FIRST THING IN THE MORNING IF AT ALL POSSIBLE, (2) PRAY BEFORE YOU READ THE PASSAGE ASKING GOD TO SPEAK TO YOU THROUGH IT, (3) LOOK FOR WAYS IN YOUR LIFE THAT NEED TO BE CHANGED TO ALLOW YOU TO BE MORE CHRISTLIKE.

TUESDAY

Pray:

☐ PRAY
☐ READ
☐ RESPOND

Read 2 Corinthians 6:14.

Who does this passage say your closest friends should be?

985003

Read 2 Corinthians 6:14 again.

Is there a relationship that you need to change because of this truth?

Commitment Prayer:

(1) SPEND TIME FIRST THING IN THE MORNING IF AT ALL POSSIBLE, (2) PRAY BEFORE YOU READ THE PASSAGE ASKING GOD TO SPEAK TO YOU THROUGH IT, (3) LOOK FOR WAYS IN YOUR LIFE THAT NEED TO BE CHANGED TO ALLOW YOU TO BE MORE CHRISTLIKE.

WEDNESDAY

☐ PRAY
☐ READ
☐ RESPOND

985003

Pray:

Read Acts 2:42-47.

What was the benefit of such a close bond between the believers?

Read Acts 2:42-47 again.

Do you think such a sharing community can exist in today's society?

Commitment Prayer:

(1) SPEND TIME FIRST THING IN THE MORNING IF AT ALL POSSIBLE, (2) PRAY BEFORE YOU READ THE PASSAGE ASKING GOD TO SPEAK TO YOU THROUGH IT, (3) LOOK FOR WAYS IN YOUR LIFE THAT NEED TO BE CHANGED TO ALLOW YOU TO BE MORE CHRISTLIKE.

THURSDAY

☐ PRAY
☐ READ
☐ RESPOND

985003

Pray:

Read 1 Corinthians 10:13.

How can an accountability partner help you find a way of escape?

Read 1 Corinthians 10:13 again.

What are some ways you have been helped by a Christian friend?

Commitment Prayer:

(1) SPEND TIME FIRST THING IN THE MORNING IF AT ALL POSSIBLE, (2) PRAY BEFORE YOU READ THE PASSAGE ASKING GOD TO SPEAK TO YOU THROUGH IT, (3) LOOK FOR WAYS IN YOUR LIFE THAT NEED TO BE CHANGED TO ALLOW YOU TO BE MORE CHRISTLIKE.

FRIDAY

Pray:

☐ PRAY
☐ READ
☐ RESPOND

Read Matthew 18:19-20.

Why do you think Jesus emphasized He is present with two or more?

985003

Read Matthew 18:19-20 again.

How could this verse affect the way you pray?

Commitment Prayer:

(1) SPEND TIME FIRST THING IN THE MORNING IF AT ALL POSSIBLE, (2) PRAY BEFORE YOU READ THE PASSAGE ASKING GOD TO SPEAK TO YOU THROUGH IT, (3) LOOK FOR WAYS IN YOUR LIFE THAT NEED TO BE CHANGED TO ALLOW YOU TO BE MORE CHRISTLIKE.

SATURDAY

Pray:

☐ PRAY
☐ READ
☐ RESPOND

Read Ephesians 5:15-21.

How can Christian friends help you make the most of every moment?

985003

Read Ephesians 5:15-21 again.

Why do you think Paul emphasized believers singing together?

Commitment Prayer:

(1) SPEND TIME FIRST THING IN THE MORNING IF AT ALL POSSIBLE, (2) PRAY BEFORE YOU READ THE PASSAGE ASKING GOD TO SPEAK TO YOU THROUGH IT, (3) LOOK FOR WAYS IN YOUR LIFE THAT NEED TO BE CHANGED TO ALLOW YOU TO BE MORE CHRISTLIKE.

MEMORY VERSES FOR THE WEEK
ECCLESIASTES 4:9-10

To help you memorize the passage this week, write it on a stick-on label and put it on your school notebook. Each time you pick up the notebook, repeat the verses again. Practice saying it to your accountability partner from memory this week.

God-sized Challenge

Meet with your accountability partner. Choose, plan, and carry out one of the following challenges together.

1. Interview a minister from another church. Ask this minister questions about the difficulty faced in his or her personal family life because of the demands of ministry. Ask the minister to also tell you what accountability means to him or her and how he or she personally practices accountability.

2. Interview police officers or fire fighters at their place of work. Ask them to discuss how important it is to have a partner. Ask them to describe a difficult situation when a partner wasn't close by. Ask: How did it feel? Did it make you do anything differently the next time? What kind of relationship exists between partners?

3. Plan an adult supervised action-adventure activity that causes you and your accountability partner to depend on each other. (Example: adult supervised rock climbing) Report to your leader the answers to these questions: What safety preparations did you both have to do? How important was it that others were with you?

PYRAMID
- on carpet
- no pyramid with no ppl.
   3 = PYRAMID!

Week-at-a-Glance

Priorities

Essentials

Sunday

MORNING	AFTERNOON	EVENING

Monday

MORNING	AFTERNOON	EVENING

Tuesday

MORNING	AFTERNOON	EVENING

Wednesday

MORNING	AFTERNOON	EVENING

Thursday

MORNING	AFTERNOON	EVENING

Friday

MORNING	AFTERNOON	EVENING

Saturday

MORNING	AFTERNOON	EVENING

Jackson ran into a youth leader from his church at the grocery store. "Jackson," she said, "where on earth have you been? I haven't seen you at church in a month. I called your house and left a message checking to see if you were sick. I'm glad to see that you are OK, but I miss you at church." Jackson nodded sheepishly. "I know," he told her. "I love being there, but I just haven't had the time. I had to get a job to pay for my new car. With the job, track practice, school, and my work with the Junior Jedi Fan Club, I hardly have time to watch TV—much less spend time with God."

Someone said we always make time for the things that are most important to us. If that is true, why is it so easy for the most important thing—your relationship with God—to get crowded out by everything else? During this session we are going to focus on setting priorities … and keeping them.

GROUP STUDY

00000000000000000000000000000000000000000000000000000000000000000000000000000000

True story: Blake's football team had just won the district championship in an incredible Saturday afternoon game at their own stadium. You can imagine how excited the guys on the team were. Blake's family was ecstatic, too. As soon as Blake got home, they were hugging him and congratulating him. "Let's go celebrate," they told him. "We'll go out to your favorite restaurant for dinner."

"Sounds great," Blake told them, "but I have something I have to do first. We can leave in about half an hour."

"What do you need to do?" his mom asked him, a little perplexed that something was more important than celebrating immediately.

"I didn't do my Bible study before I left this morning. I made a commitment to God that I was going to keep up with my Bible study everyday. I do it every afternoon. That's first priority. I'll be happy to go out and celebrate when I get done."

Does the story sound strange to you? Do you think it would have really made any difference if Blake had skipped doing his Bible study that afternoon? Why?

What Are Your Priorities?

Setting priorities is what this week's study is all about. List the five things that are your top priorities in life. This may take a little thought, so don't rush through it. You may want to talk it over with a friend or your discipleship leader.

1. _____
2. _____
3. _____
4. _____
5. _____

Did you list your top five priorities? They might change from time to time as your life changes. However, for the most part, what you make priority in your life right now as a teenager will be what you make priority in your life from now on. Try something else. What do you spend the most time on?

Setting Priorities | 031

List the top five things that occupy your time:

1. _____
2. _____
3. _____
4. _____
5. _____

Do you spend most of your time on the things that are most important to you? Or do you spend most of your time on things that really don't mean that much to you?

What's Really Important?

Jesus was big on priorities. For example, read Matthew 6:19-20.

According to these verses, what kinds of things did Jesus say not to invest your time in? Give a few examples of what you think He was talking about.

What did Jesus tell people to invest their lives in? Give a few examples of what you think He was talking about.

Earthly things or heavenly things—that's your choice. What will you establish as most important in your life?

Take a look at the list of things you could devote your life to. Mark them either "E" for earthly or "H" for heavenly.

_____ Learning the Scriptures   _____ Entertainment

_____ Fashion   _____ Worship of God

_____ Friends   _____ Sharing Christ

_____ Making money   _____ Going to school

_____ Family   _____ Attending church

Are your life priorities mostly things that are eternal or things that are earthly? It is worth thinking about.

Consider the Sparrows

I went to college with a guy named Ron. Ron was a nice guy and he was very committed to Christ. He spent tons of his time doing personal Bible study, and he led a Bible study for guys in the dorm once a week. If someone asked Ron to go see a movie with them, he would say that he didn't go to movies. If he found out a Christian friend was going to a party, Ron wanted to know why they were wasting their time going to parties when there was so much work to do for the kingdom.

GALATIANS
6:7-10

How do you feel about Ron? Is he the kind of Christian friend you would want? Why or why not?

A lot of students think that if they live their lives like Jesus told His followers to, they will never have any fun. Some students worry that if they follow Jesus, they will never get anything new and they will be forced to shop at thrift stores. (OK, some of you like shopping at thrift stores, but you understand what I mean.) Some students worry that they will never go to another party or have any friends. But that is not what Jesus taught.

Read Matthew 6:25-34 and answer these questions:
1. Why did Jesus tell His followers not to worry about having enough to eat? (v. 26)

2. How does the Bible describe the way the lilies of the field are dressed? (v. 28-29)

3. Why did Jesus say that you don't have to worry about what you eat, or what you drink, or what you wear? (v. 31-32)

4. What does the Bible tell you to do instead of seeking after all of those things that you need? (v. 33)

You need friends. You need times to relax and be entertained. You need to have people who love you. You need a family. You need clothes to wear and food to eat. Your family provides for many of those things now. You will still need those things later, which probably means that you will need a job. It just makes sense that if you need those things, you would do your best to get them. But Jesus turned human reason upside down. Instead of seeking those things that you need, Jesus said to seek His kingdom. Get this: When you seek His kingdom (desire to know, love, and obey Him), not only do you get this incredible relationship with God, but Jesus said that all of those things that you need are added as well.

Is God Your First Priority?

Would you agree or disagree with the following statement? God should be your number one priority. ☐ Agree   ☐ Disagree

Most Christians would agree that this is a true statement, but it really isn't. Are you shocked?

Here's what I mean: Jesus should not just be one of your priorities. He should be the Lord of your whole life. He is the One that should determine your priorities. Read Galatians 2:20. As a Christian, your life should be so bound up in Christ that everything you do is determined by Him.

I hope you will agree that your family should be a high priority. Why? Because they give you a place to sleep and eat. Not really. It is because God established the family and He said that your family should be of great importance to you. Your education should be a high priority. Why? Because you need to get a good job later in life. That may be true, but for a Christian that should not really be the reason. School is your vocation right now. God has made it clear that you are to do your work unto Him. You don't do school work well because it will make you smart. You do school work well because your life belongs to Christ. Should you make Bible study a high priority? Church involvement? Prayer? Of course! Why? Because Jesus placed great importance on them.

God should not be your first priority; He should be Lord of each one of your priorities!

MATTHEW
7:24-27

With all of that in mind, go back to your original list of priorities. Would you like to change any of them? If so, make your new list here:

1. _____
2. _____
3. _____
4. _____
5. _____

Living Your Priorities

MATTHEW 6:33

Someone approached you about being in this discipleship group. Did you ask yourself, do I have time for this? Jesus told us to count the cost before we determine to follow Him. (See Matt. 16:24-25.) On the other hand, you will never have the time to do anything unless you make the time.

At 5:30 a.m. every weekday, I am at the gym for my morning workout. I know, some of you are dying at the thought that anyone but God is up at 5:30 in the morning. The truth is, I'm not really a morning person. I would rather be asleep at 5:30, too. But I know that I need exercise to perform my best. I would like to do it later in the day, but I have discovered that something always comes up. Now, I'm not telling you to

get up and exercise at 5:30 in the morning, but I am saying that if you are going to make anything a priority, it won't just happen. You will have to plan and make time for it.

Turn to the calendar on page 44. Begin by writing down the things you want to be priority in your life. They may be exactly the same as the five priorities you listed on page 31. Next, write down the essentials: a test you have to take this week, something you have already committed to do for your family, time you have to be in school.

HEBREWS 12:1-3

Next, begin planning your week with the things that are most important going in first. Leave room for the essentials, but don't begin with the essentials. Yes, studying for a test is important, but what is most important? Once you have the most important things planned, add the essential things. Finally, plan some leisure time. Leave some time open to spend with friends or to work on a favorite hobby.

Living your priorities is not easy. Some people or activities will try to plan your time for you. However, no one else will plan your schedule according to the priorities God has for your life. If you want to live for God, you will have to plan it that way yourself. Refer to your priority calendar often during the week.

ON YOUR OWN

Missionary William Carey once said, "Attempt great things for God. Expect great things from God." To attempt great things for God we need to get to know Him first! In other words, we need to spend time with Him before we do anything else.

MATTHEW 14:23

Take a look at the example of Jesus. Read Matthew 14:13. There were always so many people who wanted to see Jesus. There were always people who wanted His help. You might think that the godly thing to do would be to hang with hurting people all the time and try to meet as many needs as He could. And yet, that isn't what Jesus did. He pulled away and spent time alone with God. Why?

Here's a hint: Look at the Scripture reference again. What event took place right after Jesus withdrew to a solitary place?

When we spend time with God, He is better able to equip us to live a life that is exciting, challenging, and victorious! What we do with our time really shows what is important to us. Our priorities should dictate how we spend our time.

Let's take a look at some of life's priorities. Rank these in the order that you actually live by in terms of importance, with 1 being what you spend the most time doing, and so on.
___ School
___ Friends
___ Family
___ Personal prayer and Bible study
___ Hobbies or fun activities
___ Church life and church activities

MATTHEW 6:24

Does your schedule reflect your priorities? As you evaluate each area, you might find that your actions and time spent aren't exactly in line with the numbers that you listed above. This should remind you that each week you must take an intentional look at what is important in your life and then prioritize it. Once you take the time to do that, you can plan your week according to what is most important rather than being caught up in a busy cycle that never reflects your priorities.

Next, evaluate how you are doing in the time you spend and the choices you make in the areas listed above.

SCHOOL: School is an important part of life! Are you making it a priority? Are you giving it your best? Read 1 Corinthians 10:31.

FRIENDS: The friends you hang with are the ones who influence you the most. Think of your two or three closest friends. Is their influence on you helping you grow in your relationship with Christ?
(check one) ❑ Yes   ❑ Somewhat   ❑ No

If your friends are not helping you in your walk with Christ, you need to consider finding other friends that will help you be more Christlike.

FAMILY: What kind of time are you spending with your family?

Families can only grow closer if they actually spend time together. You may see your family as an embarrassment or an inconvenience. Be careful, that is never the way God describes the family.

PERSONAL PRAYER AND BIBLE STUDY: It takes time to have a growing relationship with Christ. Prayer, Bible study, and involvement in church are essential if you want to walk with Christ. How would you rate your time with God? (check one)
❑ Vibrant and growing   ❑ OK, but nothing to shout about
❑ Pretty much nothing there

HOBBIES OR FUN ACTIVITIES: Video games, sports, music, art ... what makes you tick? List what you enjoy doing whenever you get free time.

How much time do you spend per week involved in your hobby or fun activities?

Does this crowd out other priorities, or do you seem to have a good balance?

CHURCH LIFE AND ACTIVITIES: Sunday School, discipleship, music, missions, worship, outreach . . . wow! That's a lot! Each of these activities are important, but how can you fit all of them into one week?

HEBREWS 10:25

It is important that we see how the different church activities can help us grow in our personal relationship with Christ. But be careful not to equate being busy at church with spiritual growth. Church activities in some ways are like your other activities; determine your reason for participating in an activity. I'm not saying throw church activities out of your schedule, I am saying allow God to schedule your priorities.

List three ways you can be more intentional in getting the most out of your church activities?

1. _____

_____

2. _____

_____

3. _____

_____

Read Hebrews 12:1-3 to see a great picture of how you can run the race in becoming more like Jesus. What you must do is:
1. Throw off the things that are weighing you down.
2. Persevere and run the race as it is marked.
3. Fix your eyes on Jesus.
4. Remember what Jesus went through so you don't lose heart.

List the things that are weighing you down right now.

Pray asking God to help you throw off the things you identified that are weighing you down.

Now that you have identified your priorities (marked the course) are you willing to keep on keeping on with your priorities? Stop right now and write a prayer to God asking Him to help you persevere and run the race as it is marked.

Are your eyes fixed on Jesus?

Read Hebrews 12:2-3 again. Pray, thanking God for Jesus who endured so much for you.

CHARACTER TRAIT STUDY

{ **Self-control—** The ability to control one's impulses, especially in the areas of thought life, words you say, relationships with the opposite sex, and how you spend your time. }

Galatians 5:22-23 identifies self-control as a fruit of the Spirit. You can develop the Spirit's fruit in your life by practicing obedience to God, prayer, and staying in His Word. When you want to do something other than God's will, be obedient to the Spirit. That's the start of self-control.

List three ways self-control will help you to spend your time on priorities in the upcoming week?

1. _____

2. _____

3. _____

SUNDAY

☐ PRAY
☐ READ
☐ RESPOND

985003

Pray:

Read Galatians 6:7-10.

What are some "seeds" that you have been planting in this past year?

Read Galatians 6:7-10 again.

How can you avoid getting weary of doing good?

Commitment Prayer:

(1) SPEND TIME FIRST THING IN THE MORNING IF AT ALL POSSIBLE, (2) PRAY BEFORE YOU READ THE PASSAGE ASKING GOD TO SPEAK TO YOU THROUGH IT, (3) LOOK FOR WAYS IN YOUR LIFE THAT NEED TO BE CHANGED TO ALLOW YOU TO BE MORE CHRISTLIKE.

MONDAY

Pray:

☐ PRAY
☐ READ
☐ RESPOND

Read Hebrews 10:25.

Why is it important for us to meet with other Christians on a regular basis?

Read Hebrews 10:25 again.

Who are you encouraging this week? How?

Commitment Prayer:

985003

(1) SPEND TIME FIRST THING IN THE MORNING IF AT ALL POSSIBLE, (2) PRAY BEFORE YOU READ THE PASSAGE ASKING GOD TO SPEAK TO YOU THROUGH IT, (3) LOOK FOR WAYS IN YOUR LIFE THAT NEED TO BE CHANGED TO ALLOW YOU TO BE MORE CHRISTLIKE.

TUESDAY

Pray:

☐ PRAY
☐ READ
☐ RESPOND

Read Matthew 7:24-27.

What foundation have you been building on?

Read Matthew 7:24-27 again.

What do you need to do differently to prepare for the storms of life?

Commitment Prayer:

985003

(1) SPEND TIME FIRST THING IN THE MORNING IF AT ALL POSSIBLE, (2) PRAY BEFORE YOU READ THE PASSAGE ASKING GOD TO SPEAK TO YOU THROUGH IT, (3) LOOK FOR WAYS IN YOUR LIFE THAT NEED TO BE CHANGED TO ALLOW YOU TO BE MORE CHRISTLIKE.

WEDNESDAY

☐ PRAY
☐ READ
☐ RESPOND

985003

Pray:

Read Matthew 14:23.

Why did Jesus get away from the crowd?

Read Matthew 14:23 again.

What can you do this week to follow Jesus' example?

Commitment Prayer:

(1) SPEND TIME FIRST THING IN THE MORNING IF AT ALL POSSIBLE, (2) PRAY BEFORE YOU READ THE PASSAGE ASKING GOD TO SPEAK TO YOU THROUGH IT, (3) LOOK FOR WAYS IN YOUR LIFE THAT NEED TO BE CHANGED TO ALLOW YOU TO BE MORE CHRISTLIKE.

THURSDAY

☐ PRAY
☐ READ
☐ RESPOND

985003

Pray:

Read Matthew 6:24.

What evidence is there in your life that you are serving Christ?

Read Matthew 6:24 again.

What in your life sometimes pulls you away from Christ?

Commitment Prayer:

(1) SPEND TIME FIRST THING IN THE MORNING IF AT ALL POSSIBLE, (2) PRAY BEFORE YOU READ THE PASSAGE ASKING GOD TO SPEAK TO YOU THROUGH IT, (3) LOOK FOR WAYS IN YOUR LIFE THAT NEED TO BE CHANGED TO ALLOW YOU TO BE MORE CHRISTLIKE.

FRIDAY

Pray:

☐ PRAY
☐ READ
☐ RESPOND

Read Hebrews 12:1-3

What hinders you from fully living for Christ?

985003

Read Hebrews 12:1-3 again.

How can you shed that hindrance?

Commitment Prayer:

(1) SPEND TIME FIRST THING IN THE MORNING IF AT ALL POSSIBLE, (2) PRAY BEFORE YOU READ THE PASSAGE ASKING GOD TO SPEAK TO YOU THROUGH IT, (3) LOOK FOR WAYS IN YOUR LIFE THAT NEED TO BE CHANGED TO ALLOW YOU TO BE MORE CHRISTLIKE.

SATURDAY

Pray:

☐ PRAY
☐ READ
☐ RESPOND

Read Matthew 6:33.

Do you treat anything as if it were of more importance than Christ?

985003

Read Matthew 6:33 again.

How can you seek God's kingdom first?

Commitment Prayer:

(1) SPEND TIME FIRST THING IN THE MORNING IF AT ALL POSSIBLE, (2) PRAY BEFORE YOU READ THE PASSAGE ASKING GOD TO SPEAK TO YOU THROUGH IT, (3) LOOK FOR WAYS IN YOUR LIFE THAT NEED TO BE CHANGED TO ALLOW YOU TO BE MORE CHRISTLIKE.

MEMORY VERSE FOR THE WEEK
HEBREWS 12:1

Write each word of the verse on a different index card. Lay them out on the floor in front of you. Then, turn them over one at a time. See how many you can turn over and still be able to say the verse.

God-sized Challenge

Meet with your accountability partner and together choose and complete one of the following challenges. Be prepared to share the results at your next group meeting.

1. Find one thing that you and your partner watch on TV each week. Your challenge is to meet together during that one hour, skip watching TV, use the entire hour to each share with the other how you became a Christian and talk about the struggles that you have now in trying to live the Christian life.

2. Find a fitness trainer to interview. Ask these questions:
   • What are the most important components to developing a healthy body?
   • How often do you need to watch your diet?
   • How often should you work out?
   • What keeps people from staying with their fitness plan?
   After the interview, talk with your partner about how the demands for a healthy spiritual body are very similar to that of a healthy physical body. It takes time and it must be a priority. Prepare a poster illustrating the similarities and conclusion.

3. Conduct a survey at your school with at least 10 classmates to find out their top five priorities. In the survey be sure to find out: 1. Their top five priorities; 2. How often these priorities change; 3. If there are some priorities that don't change.
   This survey can be done by doing a one-to-one question and answer time, or you can create a simple form for them to fill out. Be prepared to share your conclusions related to the survey with your group at the next meeting.

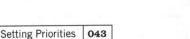

Week-at-a-Glance

Priorities   ## Essentials

Sunday

MORNING	AFTERNOON	EVENING

Monday

MORNING	AFTERNOON	EVENING

Tuesday

MORNING	AFTERNOON	EVENING

Wednesday

MORNING	AFTERNOON	EVENING

Thursday

MORNING	AFTERNOON	EVENING

Friday

MORNING	AFTERNOON	EVENING

Saturday

MORNING	AFTERNOON	EVENING

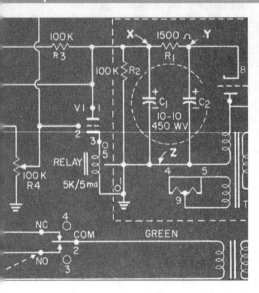

Don't you love those old movies where people are looking for buried treasure? They sail over treacherous seas and battle pirates, but they finally find the treasure and open the treasure chest. You watch the eyes of the hero get big as the treasure is opened. Of course, in most of those movies, it never works out for the hero to keep the treasure. For whatever reason, the treasure usually ends up back at the bottom of the sea. What is that about? It reminds me of the way most Christians handle Scripture. We open the Bible, an incredible store of riches from the very mouth of God. But then, for whatever reason, we often put it on a shelf without wrapping our fingers around a single jewel of a truth. Get ready, because this session will be a treasure hunt. And we aren't putting this treasure back.

GROUP STUDY

○○○
○○○
○○○

"I just don't get anything out of the Bible," Kim said. The statement left Rocky with his mouth open. He and Kim attended a Bible study every week. The Bible just seemed to explode in Rocky's mind. Every verse he read seemed to speak volumes to his heart. Rocky couldn't believe that Kim didn't get anything out of Scripture.

Why is it that some people draw such meaning and hope from the Bible while other people see it as useless for their lives? Even Christians sometimes struggle to experience real meaning from Scripture. You see, the Bible is not just an old book about God; it is a Book that was uniquely inspired by God. It is the very Word of God.

2 PETER
1:20-21

Read 1 Corinthians 2:14. According to this verse, how does someone understand something that comes from God?

Studying the Bible is not so much digging out the truth. It is more allowing God's Spirit to reveal truth. The Bible is not a matter of personal interpretation. (See 2 Pet. 3:16.)

Read John 14:26 and answer the following questions.
Who did Jesus say God would send to you?

What did Jesus say this Person would do for you?

The key is to allow the Holy Spirit to be your guide as you discover the truths of God. He will apply the truth of God to the specific situations of your life.

JOHN 8:31-32

How does this happen? How can you experience the truths of Scripture from the guidance of the Holy Spirit? There is no magic formula. But if the Holy Spirit is not your teacher, the Bible will always seem dry and will not seem to make any true difference in your life. Here are some suggestions for how to approach the Bible with the Holy Spirit as your teacher.

Tips for Studying God's Word

1. _____ before reading God's Word. (See John 14:26.) Ask God to teach you from His Word. Recently, I took a photography class at a local college. There were a lot of students in the class who just wanted an easy elective. I wanted to learn all I could. In fact, I told my instructor, "I really want to learn to take better pictures. Please, teach me what makes a picture good." She would point out the elements in my photographs that made them good so that I could keep doing them. More importantly, she would tell me how to correct poor elements in my photos. She worked hard to teach me because I asked her to. Much more than a college instructor, the Holy Spirit desires to teach you. He longs to help you live out the godly principles of Scripture. If you ask Him, He will teach you.

PSALM
119:15-16

2. _____ the Scripture passage slowly. _____ it more than once. God's Words are given to all of God's people to help them. In Acts 17:11-12 we learn about the Bereans. Paul presented the gospel to them, but they didn't just accept this new teaching. They began a daily examination of the Old Testament Scriptures to see if Paul's teachings were true. God's desire is that we examine the Bible and linger over His Words to us. When you do, He will reveal great truth to you.

Read Acts 17:11-12. When was the last time you eagerly read the Bible? What was the reason for your eagerness?

3. Pay attention to the _____ of Scripture. There is an old joke about a man who was looking for guidance from the Bible. He opened his Bible, put his finger on a verse and read, "Judas went out and hanged himself." He was not sure that was the direction he was looking for, so he tried again. This time he read, "Go ye and do likewise." A little fearful, he tried one more time: "What you do, do quickly." Reading verses out of context can be dangerous if we want to know truth. Don't read verses in isolation. Here's an example:

Read Proverbs 4:21 without looking at any other verses around it. It sounds important, but what is the *them* in the verse? Now read Proverbs 4:20 and 22. What is God saying to you in these verses?

It is important to understand the thoughts that lead up to a statement, and the thoughts that follow it. You probably know John 3:16. To whom did Jesus speak those words? What was the situation?

4. Ask yourself: What does this verse or statement _____? (See 2 Tim. 2:15.) One of the oldest forms of humor is when two people are talking but they each mean something different by the words they are using. Have you ever seen the old Abbott and Costello sketch, "Who's on First?" It gets really confusing because the player on first base has the unusual name of "Who." When Lou asks, "Who's on first?" Bud responds, "Yes." If you want to know what Exodus 20:12 means, you will have to find out what the Bible means by the word *honor*.

You also may need to understand the customs during the time in which the Bible was written. For example, John 13:1-17 talks about Jesus washing the feet of His disciples. That might seem kind of strange unless you understand that washing the feet of guests before a meal was an important tradition. Who usually washed the feet? The leader of the group? Never. That was the job of a slave.

How do you discover those answers? It may not be as difficult as you think. As you read, write down questions that you have about words, sayings, or events. Then, either ask a youth leader about them or look them up in a Bible dictionary or commentary. Your Bible might even have notes that will answer some of your questions.

5. Ask yourself: How can I _____ _____ this truth in my life? (See 2 Tim. 3:16.) If you are like me, you probably have heard the story of Peter walking on the water to Jesus about 100 times. (See Matt. 14:22-33.) Suddenly, one day it hit me: Peter got out of the boat! He did something unbelievably risky. He put his life completely in God's hands. I started wondering, *How can I trust Jesus the way Peter did when he stepped out of the boat?*

1 CORINTHIANS 10:13

Bible study is about more than knowing what John 10:10 says. Bible study means allowing the Holy Spirit to teach you how you can apply the teaching to your life. As you read a passage of Scripture, ask yourself:
- Is there an example for me to follow?
- Is there a command to obey?
- Is there a promise I can claim?
- Is there a warning I can use?

Make sure to ask the Holy Spirit how the passage you are studying applies to your life, then listen to His answer.

6. _____ what the Word says. (See Jas. 1:22.) In the old movies about knights of the round table, a knight would lay his sword before the king. By doing this he was saying, "I am at your disposal. I will fight for you to the death, tell me where to go and what to do." Most of us want God to tell us what He wants us to do, then we will decide

JAMES 1:22

whether or not we will do it. That is not the kind of obedience God is looking for. That is not obedience at all. He is looking for Christians who will lay their swords before His throne. When you see God's direction for you in His Word, the only appropriate response is to pick up your sword and do exactly what God has told you to do.

Do you remember when you were learning to write? You used that great big pencil that barely fit in your hand. With your tongue sticking out of the side of your mouth, you concentrated on each letter. Writing a simple word like *dog* or *cat* could be several minutes of work. Now, you don't even think about how to write a word. (Well, until you have to write a word like *antidisestablishmentarianism.)*

COLOSSIANS
3:16

The same is true whenever you learn anything new. You have to slow down and think about it. Right now, studying the Bible may seem like hard work. It may seem easier just to wait until you get to youth group meeting and let the youth leader tell you what the Bible means. Don't do it. Spend some time digging into the Word for yourself. As you spend time in the Word, you will find that the Holy Spirit guides you into a greater relationship with God.

You will find that approaching God's Word seems less confusing the more time you spend in it.

ON YOUR OWN

You are in the hospital to get your tonsils taken out. Your sweet Sunday School teacher doesn't know that a teenager would rather have a pizza than a house plant, so she brings you ivy. She tells you that it will remind you of how you are supposed to grow in Christ. So, you take it home. In one week, it's dead. What does that mean for your spiritual life? A lot of Christians seem to wither almost as fast as your ivy. Let's take a look at a Scripture passage that gives you a hint as to why.

Read Mark 4:1-20.
According to Jesus, what was the seed in His story? (vv.13-14)

What was the problem with the first kind of soil?

When you read verse 15, you find out that Satan came to take the Word away; it never took root.

Describe a person who responds to the Word of God like the first kind of soil.

Did you describe one who doesn't allow God's Word to penetrate his heart? **What was the problem with the second kind of soil (vv. 5-6)?**

Read verses 16-17. Jesus told the disciples the soil was rocky and seed sown on rocky places hear the Word with joy, but then trouble comes and they forget about the Word. **Describe a person who responds to the Word of God like the second kind of soil.**

What was the problem with the third kind of soil?

In verses 18-19, Jesus said this soil is full of thorns. If a seed falls in this soil, the desire for wealth and the world chokes out a desire to obey God. **Describe a person who responds to the Word of God like the third kind of soil.**

What was different about the fourth kind of soil?

ROMANS 10:17

Reread verse 20. Jesus said this soil is fertile and allows God's Word to grow and produce fruit. **Describe a person who responds to the Word of God like the fourth kind of soil.**

Which kind of soil would you say your life is?
❏ **impenetrable**   ❏ **full of rocks**   ❏ **full of thorns**   ❏ **fertile**

If you want God's Word to take root in your life and grow, you will need to cultivate the soil. Seek to have the kind of openness to God that allows His Word to take deep root in you. Each week you are memorizing a verse of Scripture. That is really the best way to allow Scripture to take root in your life. As you read, study, memorize, and hear the Word of God, allow the Spirit to change your life with the message.

CHARACTER TRAIT STUDY

> **Joy—** The ability to have peace in every situation. Joy differs from happiness in that happiness is dependent upon circumstances while joy can be present in any situation because of the presence of Christ.

Many people associate happiness with joy. However, while happiness is based on the circumstances that surround us, we can have real joy in our lives through God's presence. One of the most significant ways of living in God's presence—and having real joy—is by being grounded in His Word. This can only come by making the Bible a vital part of our lives.

List one way you plan to make the Bible a vital part of your life on an ongoing basis as a result of today's study.

SUNDAY

QUIET TIME No. 1

Pray:

☐ PRAY
☐ READ
☐ RESPOND

Read Colossians 3:16.
How can you let the Word of Christ "dwell in you richly"?

Read Colossians 3:16 again.
How does the Word of Christ relate to singing songs?

Commitment Prayer:

985003

(1) SPEND TIME FIRST THING IN THE MORNING IF AT ALL POSSIBLE, (2) PRAY BEFORE YOU READ THE PASSAGE ASKING GOD TO SPEAK TO YOU THROUGH IT, (3) LOOK FOR WAYS IN YOUR LIFE THAT NEED TO BE CHANGED TO ALLOW YOU TO BE MORE CHRISTLIKE.

MONDAY

□ PRAY
□ READ
□ RESPOND

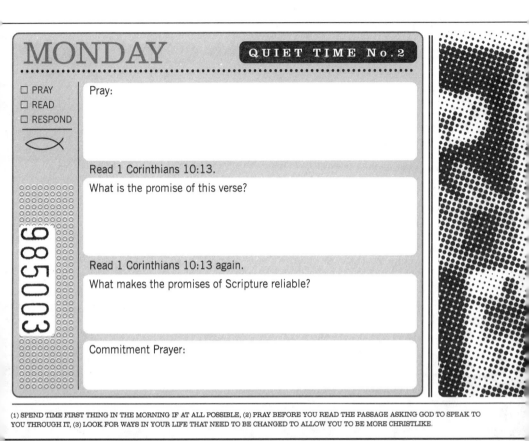

985003

Pray:

Read 1 Corinthians 10:13.
What is the promise of this verse?

Read 1 Corinthians 10:13 again.
What makes the promises of Scripture reliable?

Commitment Prayer:

(1) SPEND TIME FIRST THING IN THE MORNING IF AT ALL POSSIBLE, (2) PRAY BEFORE YOU READ THE PASSAGE ASKING GOD TO SPEAK TO YOU THROUGH IT, (3) LOOK FOR WAYS IN YOUR LIFE THAT NEED TO BE CHANGED TO ALLOW YOU TO BE MORE CHRISTLIKE.

TUESDAY

□ PRAY
□ READ
□ RESPOND

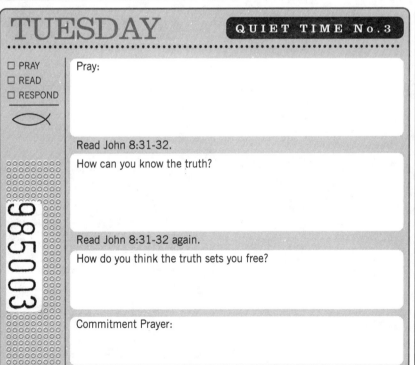

985003

Pray:

Read John 8:31-32.
How can you know the truth?

Read John 8:31-32 again.
How do you think the truth sets you free?

Commitment Prayer:

(1) SPEND TIME FIRST THING IN THE MORNING IF AT ALL POSSIBLE, (2) PRAY BEFORE YOU READ THE PASSAGE ASKING GOD TO SPEAK TO YOU THROUGH IT, (3) LOOK FOR WAYS IN YOUR LIFE THAT NEED TO BE CHANGED TO ALLOW YOU TO BE MORE CHRISTLIKE.

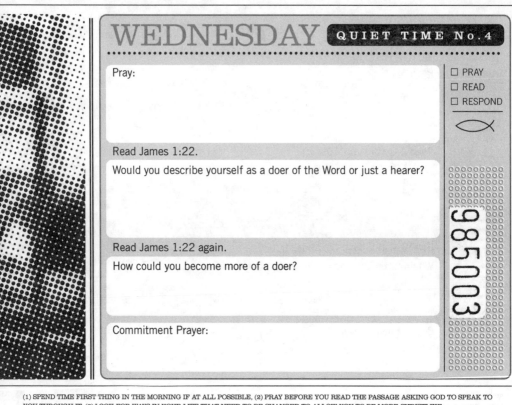

WEDNESDAY

Pray:

☐ PRAY
☐ READ
☐ RESPOND

985003

Read James 1:22.

Would you describe yourself as a doer of the Word or just a hearer?

Read James 1:22 again.

How could you become more of a doer?

Commitment Prayer:

(1) SPEND TIME FIRST THING IN THE MORNING IF AT ALL POSSIBLE, (2) PRAY BEFORE YOU READ THE PASSAGE ASKING GOD TO SPEAK TO YOU THROUGH IT, (3) LOOK FOR WAYS IN YOUR LIFE THAT NEED TO BE CHANGED TO ALLOW YOU TO BE MORE CHRISTLIKE.

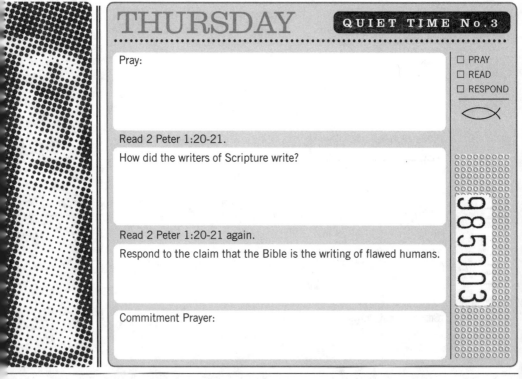

THURSDAY

Pray:

☐ PRAY
☐ READ
☐ RESPOND

985003

Read 2 Peter 1:20-21.

How did the writers of Scripture write?

Read 2 Peter 1:20-21 again.

Respond to the claim that the Bible is the writing of flawed humans.

Commitment Prayer:

(1) SPEND TIME FIRST THING IN THE MORNING IF AT ALL POSSIBLE, (2) PRAY BEFORE YOU READ THE PASSAGE ASKING GOD TO SPEAK TO YOU THROUGH IT, (3) LOOK FOR WAYS IN YOUR LIFE THAT NEED TO BE CHANGED TO ALLOW YOU TO BE MORE CHRISTLIKE.

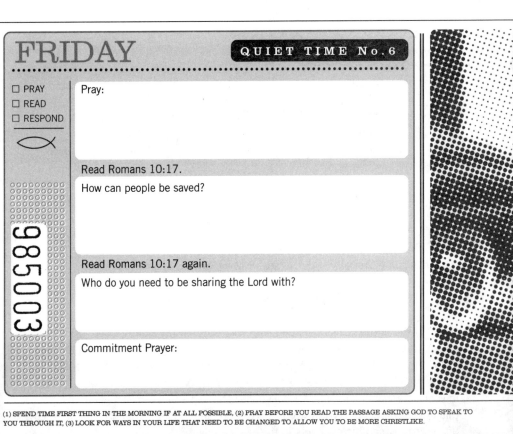

FRIDAY

QUIET TIME No. 6

☐ PRAY
☐ READ
☐ RESPOND

985003

Pray:

Read Romans 10:17.
How can people be saved?

Read Romans 10:17 again.
Who do you need to be sharing the Lord with?

Commitment Prayer:

(1) SPEND TIME FIRST THING IN THE MORNING IF AT ALL POSSIBLE, (2) PRAY BEFORE YOU READ THE PASSAGE ASKING GOD TO SPEAK TO YOU THROUGH IT, (3) LOOK FOR WAYS IN YOUR LIFE THAT NEED TO BE CHANGED TO ALLOW YOU TO BE MORE CHRISTLIKE.

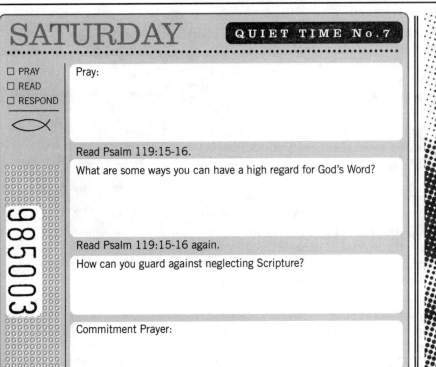

SATURDAY

QUIET TIME No. 7

☐ PRAY
☐ READ
☐ RESPOND

985003

Pray:

Read Psalm 119:15-16.
What are some ways you can have a high regard for God's Word?

Read Psalm 119:15-16 again.
How can you guard against neglecting Scripture?

Commitment Prayer:

(1) SPEND TIME FIRST THING IN THE MORNING IF AT ALL POSSIBLE, (2) PRAY BEFORE YOU READ THE PASSAGE ASKING GOD TO SPEAK TO YOU THROUGH IT, (3) LOOK FOR WAYS IN YOUR LIFE THAT NEED TO BE CHANGED TO ALLOW YOU TO BE MORE CHRISTLIKE.

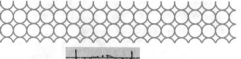

MEMORY VERSES FOR THE WEEK
2 TIMOTHY 3:16-17

Someone once said that there are three keys to successful Scripture memory. The principles are review, review, and review. You can practice the verse until you have it down. If that's all you do and someone asks you to quote the verse a week later, you probably won't be able to come up with a single phrase. Spend a little time every day going over all of your verses. Review, review, and review again.

God-sized Challenge

1. Study the entire Book of 1 Peter with your partner. It's a short book, but it will take a little time. Make a notebook for your notes from your study of 1 Peter. Take turns reading the book from two or three different Bible translations. As one of you reads, the other should make notes about what the verse says. Include your notes in your notebook. Make a list of questions you have about the verse and include this in your notebook. (What words are you not sure about? What statements seem unclear? How can the concepts in this book apply to life today?) Leave space for answers to those questions as God reveals them through additional Bible study. With your partner, write one statement that summarizes what the Book of 1 Peter is about. Include the statement in your notebook. Keep the notebook where you can find it, and when you have future Bible studies on 1 Peter, add those to your notebook. Later, you may develop a notebook for other books of the Bible.

2. Assume that someone asks you to prove that the Bible is true. Work with your partner to develop a list of proofs of the Bible. Use tools such as a Bible encyclopedia, computer software, the Internet, commentaries, Bible dictionaries, and archeological supplements. Your church library probably has all of these resources. Here are a few questions to help you get started: Is the Bible refuted by archeological finds? How have Christians throughout history viewed the Bible? Is that important? What would the world be like if everyone followed the teachings of the Bible? How did the Bible come into being? Who wrote it? Does it matter who wrote the Bible?

Week-at-a-Glance

Priorities

Essentials

Sunday

MORNING	AFTERNOON	EVENING

Monday

MORNING	AFTERNOON	EVENING

Tuesday

MORNING	AFTERNOON	EVENING

Wednesday

MORNING	AFTERNOON	EVENING

Thursday

MORNING	AFTERNOON	EVENING

Friday

MORNING	AFTERNOON	EVENING

Saturday

MORNING	AFTERNOON	EVENING

REACHING UP IN PRAYER   ΙΧΘΥΣ

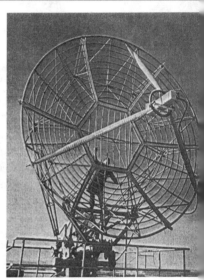

Several years ago, a Christian camp booked a famous Christian recording artist to do a concert. He brought his family to the camp, including a teenage son. After the concert, he, his son, and the camp leaders were standing in a hallway behind the auditorium. A young girl rounded the corner and walked right into the famous singer. Obviously a big fan, she took a step back and began to hyperventilate, saying over and over again, "Oh! Oh my! Oh!" The teenage son started to laugh out loud at her. To him, this Christian music icon was just dad.

When we approach God, we should be filled with love and awe. It's not the kind of silly idol worship the girl was expressing as she turned blue. God is our Father and wants us to approach Him as we would a father—not like spoiled children who demand their own way, but as loving children who delight to crawl into daddy's lap and look up into his face. So how do you crawl into your Heavenly Father's lap and look up into His face? We're going to take a look at that this week.

GROUP STUDY

Tia and Suz were the best of friends. Before school each day they would meet at the cafeteria, get something to drink, and talk nonstop until the bell rang for first period. Tia was an only child and loved hearing stories about Suz's big family. Suz couldn't wait to hear about the conversations that Tia had each night with her boyfriend, Colby. Tia and Suz loved their time together and loved sharing their lives with each other.

Karyn and Jillian also claimed to be best friends, but they got tired of each other pretty fast. Karyn loved to talk about the boys she liked, but Jillian usually was jealous of Karyn's popularity, and wouldn't listen to her. Jillian didn't tell Karyn much of what was going on in her life. Her family life was a mess; her parents were talking about divorce ... yelling about it, actually. She just didn't think Karyn would care.

What is the difference in these two friendships?

1 THESS.
5:16-20

The best friendships are the ones filled with trust. It is a wonderful thing to be able to share your life with someone else—the good times and the bad times. Friends like that can be pretty hard to find. Have you come to the point where you realize that God desires to be just that kind of friend to you? He is always there to listen. He speaks too, though it is different than speaking to another person. See if you can complete the following sentence:

Prayer is about a _____ with God and not just about a _____ made to God.

If a non-Christian friend asks you why you pray, what would your response be?

If that same friend wanted to know how to pray, what would you say?

Five Kinds of Prayer

On pages 61-62 you will learn about five different types of prayer. Fill in the blanks as you study the Bible verses given.

1. _____ **(Ex. 15:1-8)** This kind of prayer expresses the
   greatness of who God is. When you pray this kind of prayer to God, you
   tell Him who He is to you and what His attributes are.   PSALM 54

Write down as many attributes of God as you can.

Did you write the word *praise* in the blank? You are right! Praise is used
for this kind of prayer because it is adoration of who God is—His
character, His attributes, and His person. Review the attributes of God
that you listed and add others as you complete this study.

2. _____ **(Ps. 107:1-9)** This prayer is a reflection of
   the things with which God has blessed you. God is the source
   of everything you have. It is because of God that you have
   been blessed with so many things. Acknowledge God for
   all that you have and thank Him for your blessings.

What are some ways God has blessed you?

Did you write the word *thanksgiving* in the blank? You are right! The word
thanksgiving is used for this kind of prayer because it is our gratitude
acknowledging who God is and acknowledging that everything we have is
from God. As you continue this study, make it a habit to thank God for the
things that you have.

3. _____ **(Ps. 51:1-12)** This prayer involves recognizing God's
   holiness and our unworthiness. When going to God in prayer, ask Him
   to reveal to you the sin in your life. When that sin has been shown to
   you, agree with God that you committed it. Then ask God to forgive you   1 JOHN 1:8-10
   for committing that sin against Him and to cleanse you from it.

**Are there sins that you haven't confessed to God? If so, write a word or two
that reminds you of that sin below.**

Did you write the word *confession* in the blank? You are right! The word
confess is used for this kind of prayer because it is your time to
acknowledge to God that you have sinned. This is a time when you must
be honest with God and with yourself. Now that you have been reminded

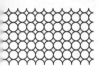

of your sin, whisper a word of confession to God. Do your best not to repeat the sin you have just confessed. Let Jesus—not sin—be the controlling guide of your life.

4. _____ **(John 17:6-19)** This kind of prayer is praying for others. God answers our prayers when we earnestly pray for others. When we are weak, the prayer of a fellow Christian can enable us to gain wisdom, knowledge, and strength we need to carry on.

Write the names of two or three others that you know need your prayers. Beside their names, write a concern they have that you can pray for.

1. _____
2. _____
3. _____

Did you write the word *intercession* in the top blank? Intercession is used for this kind of prayer because it is your request to God on someone else's behalf. Plan prayer time each day to intercede on behalf of the people you listed in the three blanks above.

5. _____ **(1 Sam. 1:9-17)** These prayers are prayers for oneself. God wants you to be honest with Him and share your heart with Him. God is pleased to hear your personal requests. He delights when you realize that you need Him. He desires to fulfill your requests when you ask according to His will. You can be thankful that God's wisdom is greater than yours—even when it comes to what you want and pray for yourself.

JOHN 15:7-8

What are some things you need? These may be material things like food or clothing, emotional things like strong friendships, or spiritual things like a closer walk with God. List a few of your requests below.

Did you write the word *petition* in the top blank? Petition is used for this kind of prayer because it is your request to God on your behalf. Each day spend time in prayer petitioning God to help you know and understand His will in a particular decision or situation you are facing.

ON YOUR OWN

Prayer may seem complicated to you, but remember that prayer is the way you communicate with God. When you became a Christian, you entered into a relationship with Him. Being a Christian is more than your ticket to heaven when you die—it is a wonderful relationship with God starting here on earth. You relate to God through prayer. He wants you to share with Him everything that's going on in your life.

Think about one of your closest friends. How do you act around him or her? What things do you talk about? What makes that person a close friend? Write that friend's name in the following space.

When you're in a relationship with God you can relate to Him the same way you relate to a close friend. Share with Him the good things and the bad things. Tell Him when you're struggling in an area of you life; don't feel like you have to hide areas of you life from Him. He already knows about them anyway!

Jesus was in constant prayer with His Father. He placed so much importance on prayer that He showed us how we are to pray. He didn't want prayer to be complicated, so He identified ways we are to pray.

MATTHEW 26:36-46

Read Matthew 6:5-15. How does Jesus specifically tell us we are to pray?

Jesus did not mean that every time we pray we are to quote this prayer. Jesus was saying that there are different facets of prayer. Examining these verses again, we can identify the different facets. Jesus calls us to praise God, thank God, confess our sin to God, pray for others, and pray for ourselves. God wants you to seek His face, draw close to Him, as you pray this week.

There may come a time in your life when you won't know how to pray or what exactly to pray for. Your heart may be burdened and when you pray you don't know exactly what to say to God. Don't get frustrated and stop praying, but instead be honest with God and tell Him you don't know what words to pray. God knows that there are times when we won't know how to pray about something.

Read Romans 8:26-27. Who is our Helper when we don't know the words to pray? How does He pray for us?

MATTHEW 6:5-6

CHARACTER TRAIT STUDY

{ **Patience—** Having the ability to wait for something without complaining. Patience is important when you pray. Even though it is natural for our human nature to want what we ask for as soon as we ask it, God answers prayers at a time and in a way that is best for us. }

Have you heard the caution, "Never pray for patience"? Often people say this because they know that patience is best learned from difficult situations or trials. Patience is not something you learn in a hurry! People with character have patience because they do not react with complaining or inappropriate, hasty behavior. The key to developing patience is striving to be aware of God's will for you, to wait on His leadership and guidance in the situations or trials you face. Pray about ways you can practice patience with others or with circumstances that may come up this week.

SUNDAY   QUIET TIME No. 1

Pray:

☐ PRAY
☐ READ
☐ RESPOND

Read Matthew 6:5-6.

What warning did Jesus give about our prayers?

985003

Read Matthew 6:5-6 again.

What is the right attitude for prayer? How can you have that attitude?

Commitment Prayer:

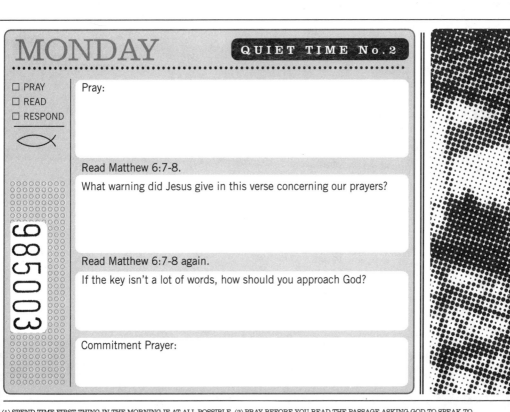

MONDAY

QUIET TIME No. 2

- ☐ PRAY
- ☐ READ
- ☐ RESPOND

985003

Pray:

Read Matthew 6:7-8.

What warning did Jesus give in this verse concerning our prayers?

Read Matthew 6:7-8 again.

If the key isn't a lot of words, how should you approach God?

Commitment Prayer:

(1) SPEND TIME FIRST THING IN THE MORNING IF AT ALL POSSIBLE, (2) PRAY BEFORE YOU READ THE PASSAGE ASKING GOD TO SPEAK TO YOU THROUGH IT, (3) LOOK FOR WAYS IN YOUR LIFE THAT NEED TO BE CHANGED TO ALLOW YOU TO BE MORE CHRISTLIKE.

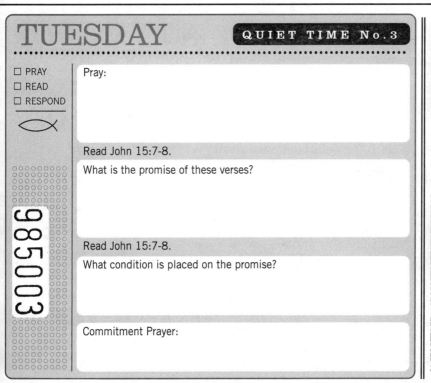

TUESDAY

QUIET TIME No. 3

- ☐ PRAY
- ☐ READ
- ☐ RESPOND

985003

Pray:

Read John 15:7-8.

What is the promise of these verses?

Read John 15:7-8.

What condition is placed on the promise?

Commitment Prayer:

(1) SPEND TIME FIRST THING IN THE MORNING IF AT ALL POSSIBLE, (2) PRAY BEFORE YOU READ THE PASSAGE ASKING GOD TO SPEAK TO YOU THROUGH IT, (3) LOOK FOR WAYS IN YOUR LIFE THAT NEED TO BE CHANGED TO ALLOW YOU TO BE MORE CHRISTLIKE.

WEDNESDAY

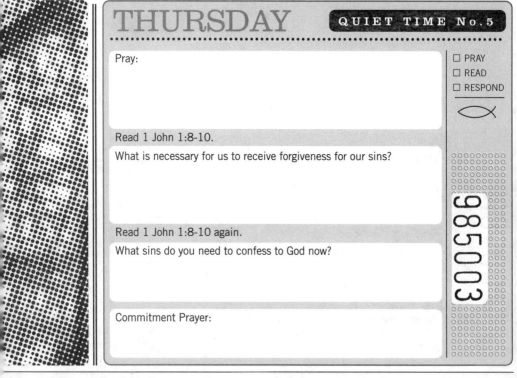

QUIET TIME No. 4

Pray:

☐ PRAY
☐ READ
☐ RESPOND

Read Psalm 54.

Can you identify with this psalm writer? When have you felt that way?

Read Psalm 54 again.

Do you automatically go to God when things are tough?

985003

Commitment Prayer:

(1) SPEND TIME FIRST THING IN THE MORNING IF AT ALL POSSIBLE, (2) PRAY BEFORE YOU READ THE PASSAGE ASKING GOD TO SPEAK TO YOU THROUGH IT, (3) LOOK FOR WAYS IN YOUR LIFE THAT NEED TO BE CHANGED TO ALLOW YOU TO BE MORE CHRISTLIKE.

THURSDAY

QUIET TIME No. 5

Pray:

☐ PRAY
☐ READ
☐ RESPOND

Read 1 John 1:8-10.

What is necessary for us to receive forgiveness for our sins?

Read 1 John 1:8-10 again.

What sins do you need to confess to God now?

985003

Commitment Prayer:

(1) SPEND TIME FIRST THING IN THE MORNING IF AT ALL POSSIBLE, (2) PRAY BEFORE YOU READ THE PASSAGE ASKING GOD TO SPEAK TO YOU THROUGH IT, (3) LOOK FOR WAYS IN YOUR LIFE THAT NEED TO BE CHANGED TO ALLOW YOU TO BE MORE CHRISTLIKE.

FRIDAY

☐ PRAY
☐ READ
☐ RESPOND

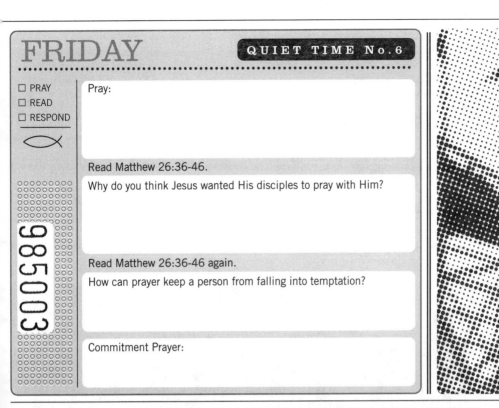

985003

Pray:

Read Matthew 26:36-46.

Why do you think Jesus wanted His disciples to pray with Him?

Read Matthew 26:36-46 again.

How can prayer keep a person from falling into temptation?

Commitment Prayer:

(1) SPEND TIME FIRST THING IN THE MORNING IF AT ALL POSSIBLE, (2) PRAY BEFORE YOU READ THE PASSAGE ASKING GOD TO SPEAK TO YOU THROUGH IT, (3) LOOK FOR WAYS IN YOUR LIFE THAT NEED TO BE CHANGED TO ALLOW YOU TO BE MORE CHRISTLIKE.

SATURDAY

☐ PRAY
☐ READ
☐ RESPOND

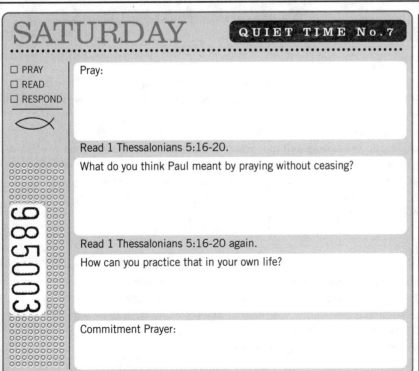

985003

Pray:

Read 1 Thessalonians 5:16-20.

What do you think Paul meant by praying without ceasing?

Read 1 Thessalonians 5:16-20 again.

How can you practice that in your own life?

Commitment Prayer:

(1) SPEND TIME FIRST THING IN THE MORNING IF AT ALL POSSIBLE, (2) PRAY BEFORE YOU READ THE PASSAGE ASKING GOD TO SPEAK TO YOU THROUGH IT, (3) LOOK FOR WAYS IN YOUR LIFE THAT NEED TO BE CHANGED TO ALLOW YOU TO BE MORE CHRISTLIKE.

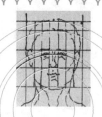

MEMORY VERSE FOR THE WEEK
JOHN 15:7

When you are trying to memorize a verse, it often helps to break it into simple phrases. Today's verse will seem much easier when you think of it as four simple phrases rather than one long verse. Memorize one phrase. Then memorize the second and add it to the first. Continue until you have the whole verse memorized.

God-sized Challenge

1. Plan a prayer walk with your accountability partner. A prayer walk is a time of praying for or about someone or something as you walk around it. To a person passing by, you won't appear to be praying, but simply walking and talking with each other. You may recall Joshua leading God's people as they marched around the city of Jericho seven days in a row. You may choose to walk around your school, a courthouse or other government building, a neighborhood, or around your church. If you choose to walk around it seven times, focus on a different prayer request during each trip. If people pass by you in a car or on the sidewalk or street, say a prayer for them as you continue your walk.

2. Have a one-hour prayer session with your accountability partner. Before you start, both partners should make a list of things to pray about. Include areas of praise, thanksgiving, confession, intercession, and petition. Have a time of both silent and audible prayer during your hour of prayer, taking turns to pray for these different areas. Try to allow the Holy Spirit to guide you to situations He wants you to pray about and ways He wants you to pray.

Week-At-A-Glance

Priorities

Essentials

Sunday

MORNING	AFTERNOON	EVENING

Monday

MORNING	AFTERNOON	EVENING

Tuesday

MORNING	AFTERNOON	EVENING

Wednesday

MORNING	AFTERNOON	EVENING

Thursday

MORNING	AFTERNOON	EVENING

Friday

MORNING	AFTERNOON	EVENING

Saturday

MORNING	AFTERNOON	EVENING

TLE
MAKING ETERNAL INVESTMENTS ΙΧΘΥΣ

There are probably times when you get stressed about things in your life. What if you don't do well on a big test? What if you've really lost your wallet this time? What if she hates you forever after what you said? I have a friend who looks at me in times of stress and says, "What difference is this going to make 10 years from now?" The truth is, most of the stuff we worry about has very little impact on the world. Autumn still follows summer. The sun still comes up in the morning. And humanity continues to thrive.

What if you could do something that would make a lasting difference? Believe it or not, you can. That's what this session is about.

GROUP SESSION

The Parable of the Two Brothers

There were once two brothers, one a year older than the other. Each day just before the father went to work, he would go into the older brother's room and give him several dollars so the two boys would have enough money for lunch at school. The father let the older brother be responsible for handling the money and giving his younger brother his share. However, the older brother never told his younger brother about the money. He would eat lunch out of sight of the younger brother while the younger brother went hungry.

You may have a brother or sister, so you know how things like this happen. How does it make you feel? How do you think the father would react if he discovered what his oldest son was doing?

Your church may take up an offering called the Lottie Moon Christmas Offering for world missions. Have you ever wondered who Lottie Moon was? Years ago, Lottie was a missionary who served in China. She grew to love the people of China. Though she missed her family and friends in the United States, she invested her life serving the people of China. During the Chinese revolution, food became scarce. Lottie continued to receive support from people in the States, and had enough to live on for herself. However, Lottie would not keep the food for herself. She took whatever she had and gave it to the poor, to children who had nothing to eat. Lottie's body became depleted and she died on her trip back home. Lottie Moon invested everything she had in ministry to other people.

Can you contrast Lottie Moon's story with the Parable of the Two Brothers? Why do you think Lottie saw the people of China as her brothers and sisters?

LUKE 9:1-6

How are you investing your life? A lot of people invest their lives in finding pleasure. Others invest their lives in obtaining money. Some people invest their lives in fame or power. Some teenagers focus all of their lives on making good grades. Others invest themselves in making their parents crazy. Think about it: In what are you investing your life?

You may say, "I'm not really investing my life in anything. I'm just trying to get by." Sometimes it feels like all you can do is get through another day. Still, Jesus talked about the importance of investing our lives. One of His parables may be the best example of investing.

Read Matthew 25:14-30.

Did you get the picture? A wealthy guy goes away on a trip. He gives each of his servants some money to invest for him. When he returns, two of them show him a profit. The third buried the money so he could give it back to the master. The master got really irritated because the third servant had done nothing with what had been entrusted to him.

Assume that the wealthy guy in this story is God. Assume that He has given His people talents that He wants them to invest. And assume that He wants a return on His investment. Assume all of this is true as you answer these questions:

I TIMOTHY 4:12-16

What has God given you that He expects you to be investing for Him?

What would it mean for you to put those things God has given you to use?

What return do you think God is looking for from what He has given you?

You probably caught on to the fact that Jesus' parable is really not about money. God certainly can give people the financial ability to help others, but God has invested so much more in us than cash. You may have great music ability, a truly caring heart, or the ability to see truth in any situation. Regardless of what God has given you, you have three choices as to what you do with it: 1. You can bury it and do nothing with it. 2. You can invest it in earthly purposes. 3. You can invest it in eternal purposes.

John was a great athlete. He was the captain of the freshman football team and was guaranteed a starting place on the varsity team as a sophomore. John also had decided that he was going to use anything God had given him to make eternal investments. He started praying with a couple of the guys on the team. After one of the toughest victories of the year, John jumped up on a bench and said that he was sure that God had allowed them to play at their best. He asked the guys on the team to kneel because he wanted to thank God. Every guy got down on his knees in the locker room as John led them in prayer.

LUKE 2:52

In the space below, list the ways that John was making eternal investments.

John used his abilities in ministry to the team. Instead of praising himself for being captain of the team, John worked hard to use the abilities that God had given him. John started a prayer group within the team. As captain of the team John knew that God had given them the abilities to play as well as they had. He gave God the credit and glory for the victory. John was not ashamed to lead his team to humble themselves and to worship God. John had his priorities right. God was his first consideration in everything he did. John was making eternal investments!

HEBREWS 11:1

Eternal Investments

Do you pay attention to the stock market? Why do people invest in stocks? Let's look at the whole picture of what happens in an investment. If someone puts money into a company, that company then has money they can use to hire employees and develop products. Those employees use the money they make and invest it in other companies ... by buying food, cars, houses. Those companies then have money to hire employees and pay them a salary. In a sense, our whole economy is built on people making investments into companies.

Making eternal investments is similar. When you invest in another person for the kingdom of God, they come to understand the love of God. Their lives can be changed for eternity. Then, they can invest in ministry. You became a Christian because someone made an investment in your life. Now you can invest in others, and as a result, God's kingdom grows.

Here's How

JAMES 1:27

If you decide that you want to invest your life in eternal things, how do you do it? Here are a few of the things the Bible says:

1. Remember to put others' needs ahead of your own. (See Phil. 2:3-4.)
2. Stay connected to God and He will guide you. (See John 15:5.)
3. Pay attention to the needs of people around you. Watch and listen for indications that someone needs a godly touch. (See Matt. 9:36-38.)
4. Minister to others without drawing attention to yourself. (See Matt. 6:2-4.)
5. Remember you are joining God in His work. You get to participate in God's eternal work, but only God makes an eternal difference in someone's life. (See John 6:44.)
6. Love other people. Most people respond positively to someone who genuinely cares about them. (See Matt. 5:43-46.)

Look up the above verses in your Bible. Briefly summarize the meaning of each passage in your own words.

ON YOUR OWN

Richard spent a lot of time working in his family's restaurant. When I invited him to church, he always had to work. I knew Richard didn't have a relationship with Jesus, but he wasn't interested when I would bring up the topic. We had been friends for about a year when Richard called me one day and I could tell by his voice that something was on his mind. When I arrived at the restaurant, Richard got right to the point and said, "I've been thinking about God and I want to follow Him. What do I do?" I prayed with Richard that day when he gave his life to Christ!

The most important eternal investment you can make is to lead someone to become a Christian. What are you saying about Jesus to your friends?

Live It Every Day

How do you approach the topic of Christ with your lost friends? It may depend on you living your faith in a way that they can see. When everyone else uses profanity, do you keep your speech clean? When they ask you why you don't drink, what you say can be a witness for Christ. When someone shares a problem, tell them you will pray for them ... and do it. If you live your faith, others will notice. Yes, some may laugh at you, but they will also come to you when they are looking for something genuine. If your faith seems fake or convenient to them, they won't be interested.

ROMANS 1:16

Explain how you are living your life with Christ every day.

Write Your Personal Salvation Experience

ACTS 20:22-24

The best way to witness to others is to share the difference Christ has made in your life. On a page 111, write your personal testimony by answering the following questions. It should be no longer than one page.
1. What was your life like before you accepted Jesus as Savior and Lord?
2. What actually happened when you accepted Jesus as Savior and Lord?
3. What has your life been like since you accepted Jesus as your Savior?

Read the gospel presentation on page 5 of this book and develop a plan to use it to share Christ with a friend. Who do you know that needs you to make the eternal investment of introducing them to Christ?

What can you do this week to begin discussing Christ with your friends?

CHARACTER TRAIT STUDY

{ **Humbleness—** Realizing your position in relation to Jesus. We must realize that He is everything and that we are nothing without Him. }

Pride and arrogance often get in the way of our humbleness. Develop an attitude of humility by becoming more Christlike in the way you think of yourself and the way you treat others. Consider in all situations what Jesus would do before you act or talk. Do you need to allow others to be first or to receive the praise? Being humble doesn't mean being weak; rather it shows your trust in God. Humbleness is more of Jesus and less of yourself. Show others Jesus through your actions this week.

SUNDAY

QUIET TIME No. 1

Pray:

☐ PRAY
☐ READ
☐ RESPOND

Read Acts 20:22-24.

What impresses you about Paul's testimony in these verses?

Read Acts 20:22-24 again.

How can you follow Paul's example?

985003

Commitment Prayer:

MONDAY

☐ PRAY
☐ READ
☐ RESPOND

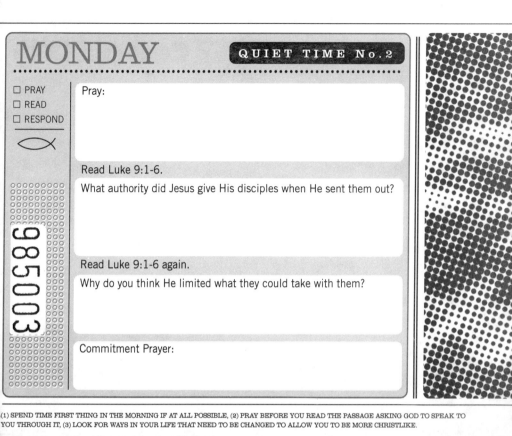

985003

Pray:

Read Luke 9:1-6.
What authority did Jesus give His disciples when He sent them out?

Read Luke 9:1-6 again.
Why do you think He limited what they could take with them?

Commitment Prayer:

(1) SPEND TIME FIRST THING IN THE MORNING IF AT ALL POSSIBLE, (2) PRAY BEFORE YOU READ THE PASSAGE ASKING GOD TO SPEAK TO YOU THROUGH IT, (3) LOOK FOR WAYS IN YOUR LIFE THAT NEED TO BE CHANGED TO ALLOW YOU TO BE MORE CHRISTLIKE.

TUESDAY

☐ PRAY
☐ READ
☐ RESPOND

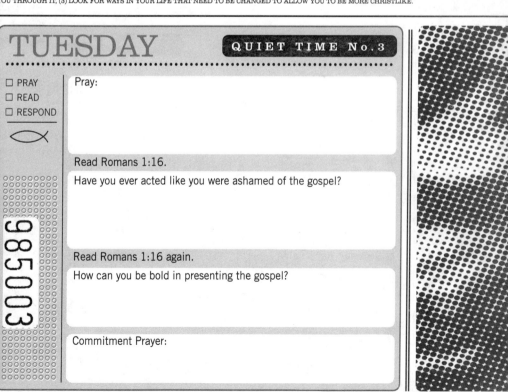

985003

Pray:

Read Romans 1:16.
Have you ever acted like you were ashamed of the gospel?

Read Romans 1:16 again.
How can you be bold in presenting the gospel?

Commitment Prayer:

) SPEND TIME FIRST THING IN THE MORNING IF AT ALL POSSIBLE, (2) PRAY BEFORE YOU READ THE PASSAGE ASKING GOD TO SPEAK TO OU THROUGH IT, (3) LOOK FOR WAYS IN YOUR LIFE THAT NEED TO BE CHANGED TO ALLOW YOU TO BE MORE CHRISTLIKE.

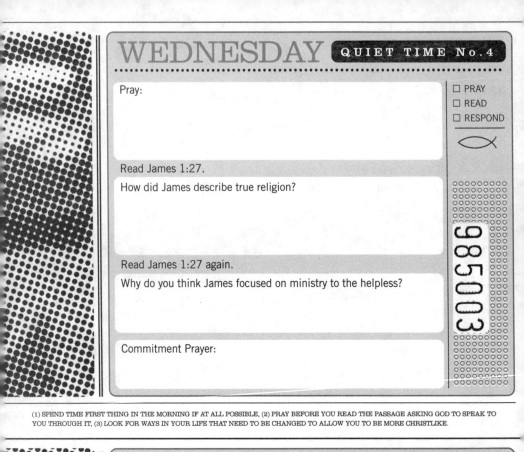

WEDNESDAY QUIET TIME No. 4

Pray:

☐ PRAY
☐ READ
☐ RESPOND

Read James 1:27.
How did James describe true religion?

Read James 1:27 again.
Why do you think James focused on ministry to the helpless?

985003

Commitment Prayer:

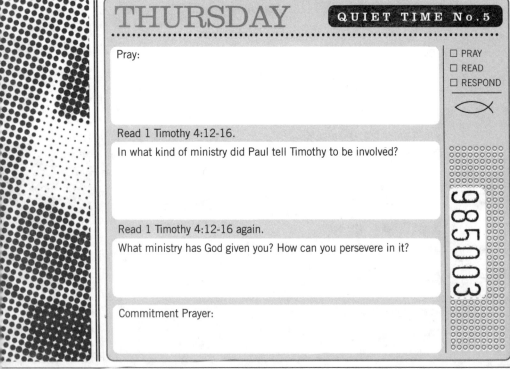

THURSDAY QUIET TIME No. 5

Pray:

☐ PRAY
☐ READ
☐ RESPOND

Read 1 Timothy 4:12-16.
In what kind of ministry did Paul tell Timothy to be involved?

Read 1 Timothy 4:12-16 again.
What ministry has God given you? How can you persevere in it?

985003

Commitment Prayer:

FRIDAY

☐ PRAY
☐ READ
☐ RESPOND

985003

Pray:

Read Hebrews 11:1.

According to this definition, do you have real faith? Why or why not?

Read Hebrews 11:1 again.

What difference does faith make in making eternal investments?

Commitment Prayer:

(1) SPEND TIME FIRST THING IN THE MORNING IF AT ALL POSSIBLE, (2) PRAY BEFORE YOU READ THE PASSAGE ASKING GOD TO SPEAK TO YOU THROUGH IT, (3) LOOK FOR WAYS IN YOUR LIFE THAT NEED TO BE CHANGED TO ALLOW YOU TO BE MORE CHRISTLIKE.

SATURDAY

☐ PRAY
☐ READ
☐ RESPOND

985003

Pray:

Read Luke 2:52.

In what ways are you growing?

Read Luke 2:52 again.

How are you more effective at ministry than you were a year ago?

Commitment Prayer:

) SPEND TIME FIRST THING IN THE MORNING IF AT ALL POSSIBLE, (2) PRAY BEFORE YOU READ THE PASSAGE ASKING GOD TO SPEAK TO OU THROUGH IT, (3) LOOK FOR WAYS IN YOUR LIFE THAT NEED TO BE CHANGED TO ALLOW YOU TO BE MORE CHRISTLIKE.

MEMORY VERSE FOR THE WEEK
ROMANS 1:16

There is something about music that makes things easier to remember. That's why you can still remember jingles you heard when you were six years old. Try putting your Scripture memory verses to music and singing them. You don't have to be a great musician. Just pick a tune like "Row, Row, Row Your Boat"—anything that seems to fit. Then, practice singing your verse to that tune.

God-sized Challenge

The Beginning of a Four-step Challenge
1. List the names of three people you would like to meet with in order to get to know them better. This could be someone who comes to church that is not actively a part of the youth group or someone who does not go to any church. Write those names here:

1._____ 2._____ 3._____

2. Get together with your accountability partner and pray for the names each of you have listed. Begin praying for at least one person each who God might want you to invite to a party at the end of this study.

The Rest of the Challenge
3. Get with your accountability partner and pray for the people on your lists. Listen as God leads you to invest some of your time in these people. Decide on a time during the next week when you and your partner will get together with the persons for whom you have been praying. The challenge for this week is for the four of you to get together for a time of fellowship, such as miniature golf, bowling, or a meal at a fast-food restaurant. Look for opportunities to tell them about Jesus and to show your beliefs through your talk, your mealtime prayer, your attitudes, and your actions.

4. Invite them to the fellowship time that will take place following the last week of this study.

Week-At-A-Glance

Priorities   Essentials

Sunday

MORNING	AFTERNOON	EVENING

Monday

MORNING	AFTERNOON	EVENING

Tuesday

MORNING	AFTERNOON	EVENING

Wednesday

MORNING	AFTERNOON	EVENING

Thursday

MORNING	AFTERNOON	EVENING

Friday

MORNING	AFTERNOON	EVENING

Saturday

MORNING	AFTERNOON	EVENING

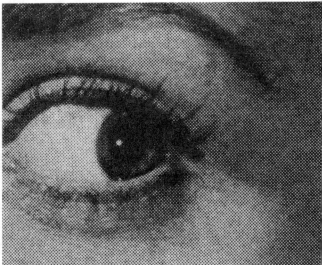

Claire laughed out loud. "Are you serious?" she asked Jerome. "You really want me to believe that there is a devil out to get me?"

Jerome took a deep breath. He wished that he hadn't told her that Satan was doing everything he could to blind her to the truth ... even though he believed it was the truth. "Look, Claire," he started cautiously, "there is more to this world than you can see."

Claire laughed again. "Yes, I know, fairies hiding under my bed, a boogie man in my closet, and a scary guy with a red suit and pitch fork lurking in the dark just waiting to jump out and scare me. Come on, Jerome. Grow up!"

Do we have a spiritual enemy or is that just a myth? Can we expect the Spirit of God to guide us through life, or do we just have to find our own way? Those are the kind of questions we're going to tackle in this session.

Driving Blind

The game is like an auto race. You control how fast your car goes and the direction. The game track has the same obstacles you would encounter on a real track. If you hit an oil slick too fast, your car spins out of control. If you take a turn too sharp, you end up in the wall. But the thing that really makes the game tough is that you can only see the road right in front of you. You have to react quickly, because you are blind to what's up ahead. Your reactions have to be quick to get a qualifying time, and your moves nearly perfect to win the race with the simulated big boys. Most players improve their scores by racing the same track until they know what's coming. Then, they can anticipate the turns and obstacles.

In a way, that's what it is like to live the Christian life. You can only see what is just ahead of you. You don't know what obstacles you will face in the next day or the next hour. The amazing thing is we have a Guide, One who knows the road. The Holy Spirit is willing to guide us through the turns and obstacles. Our choice is to listen to Him, or keep driving blind.

1 CORINTHIANS
10:13

The Voice of the Enemy

A pregnant girl might say that she and her boyfriend really were in love. A guy in rehab might explain that his first joint seemed like harmless fun; his friends and even his parents smoked. A guy who hurts people by his words might explain that he was just telling the truth and if people can't handle it, that's their problem. These people act as if sin is no big deal. The truth is that your sin has devastating consequences ... to you and to the people around you.

Read Romans 5:12. Why do people see sin as something trivial? Why do they think of immoral activity as a personal choice instead of a sin against God?

What did Jesus say about the devil? Read John 8:44.

The Bible says humanity is engaged in spiritual warfare, whether they are aware of it or not. (See Eph. 6:12.) We have a spiritual enemy. According to Jesus, Satan is a liar and the father of lies. Satan seeks to deceive people in any way that he can. People who do not know the truth of God are easily led to believe that whatever feels good at the moment must be good. Even believers can be misled by Satan's lies.

EPHESIANS
6:10-12

Read John 10:10. What is Satan's purpose? Fill in the blanks below.

Satan has come to _____ , _____ , and

_____ .

When you became a Christian, Satan lost you for eternity. He cannot take away your salvation. When you accepted Christ as your Savior, it was forever! (See 1 John 5:13.) What is Satan trying to steal from you? If you will allow him, he will steal your joy. Satan will steal your purity. Satan will steal your reputation. Satan will do anything he can to ruin you.

JOHN 10:1-10

The Voice of Truth

Read John 10:10 again. This time look at the second part of the verse. What is Jesus' purpose in our lives. Fill in the blanks below.

Jesus came so that we might have _____ and have it

_____ .

God wants you to experience an abundant life. He has set you free from that bondage and wants you to live a life free from the ugliness of sin that Satan desires for you.

Read Luke 4:1-13. How did Jesus defend Himself from Satan's temptation?

Read Matthew 26:41. What advice did Jesus give His disciples about overcoming temptation?

Jesus quoted Scripture in order to avoid temptation. He told His disciples to watch and pray. It is important to always be on guard. If you let your guard down by not seeking God consistently, you are likely to give Satan a foothold in some area of your life.

LUKE 4:1-13

On the morning of September 11, 2001, the people in the United States—the most powerful nation in the world—were not concerned about terrorism. Though the government knew that there was always a possibility that something could happen, no real action was taken to help guarantee protection from terrorists. It took the tragedy of a terrorist group hijacking airplanes and crashing them, killing thousands of United States citizens, to realize that we need to always be on guard and to develop preventative measures against the threat of terrorism.

1 CHRONICLES 7:14

Just like we realized that we need to always be on guard against terrorism, it is even more important to be on guard against Satan, for he too has come to steal, kill, and destroy.

Read 1 Peter 5:8. Are you watching and praying to guard against Satan?

ON YOUR OWN

If you were going to war, what items would you take with you? List each item and write why you chose that item.

A soldier needs equipment to fight in a physical war. To fight a spiritual war, you need spiritual weapons. God has provided exactly what you need.

Read Ephesians 6:13-18. Identify the different pieces of armor in the left column of the chart. Write how each of these pieces can be used to fight a spiritual battle.

ARMOR	WHAT IS IT?	HOW DO YOU PUT IT ON?
1. Helmet	Salvation	*Trust Christ to save you then live each day aware that you belong to Him.*
2. Belt	Truth	
3. Breastplate	Righteousness	
4. Boots	Peace	
5. Shield	Faith	
6. Sword	Word of God	

PSALM 119:105-112

Are you wearing your spiritual armor? If Satan attacks your mind by telling you to think lustfully about someone, you have the sword to protect your thoughts. Your thoughts need to line up with God's Word.

If Satan attacks your heart by telling you that you aren't good enough and you should go back to the old ways of sin, remember the breastplate of righteousness covers your heart. Christ has given you His righteousness. You are good enough because of what He has done in your life.

If Satan tries to rip you apart with lies, remember you have the belt of truth around your waist. Satan will try to deceive you, but you stand on truth.

LUKE 6:46-49

God desires for you to walk with Him. He has given you what you need to do it. Will you fail? At times, yes, but when you do, ask for His forgiveness and get back in the battle. Don't become a casualty of spiritual war. Put on the full armor of God and stay in the battle.

CHARACTER TRAIT STUDY

{ **Single-mindedness—** Giving close attention to Christ, His commands, His Person, and His ways. Focusing on Christ and not being led away by our evil desires or overcome with Satan's schemes. }

The Mind of Christ, Youth Edition by T. W. Hunt and Claude King, states that one of our spiritual problems is becoming distracted from Christ. We are led astray because our minds are bombarded with so many distractions. Single-mindedness is the trait that means we are focused on Christ. As a Christian, you can direct and control your attention with a focus on Christ. Develop this character trait by ridding your life of trivial things that demand your attention. It could mean not answering your telephone when you are in the middle of your quiet time. Deliberately focus your mind on Jesus as often as possible during the day.

SUNDAY

QUIET TIME No. 1

- ☐ PRAY
- ☐ READ
- ☐ RESPOND

985003

Pray:

Read Ephesians 6:10-12.
Which weapon is the only offensive weapon?

Read Ephesians 6:10-12 again.
Describe ways you can use the Word of God as a weapon in your life.

Commitment Prayer:

(1) SPEND TIME FIRST THING IN THE MORNING IF AT ALL POSSIBLE, (2) PRAY BEFORE YOU READ THE PASSAGE ASKING GOD TO SPEAK TO YOU THROUGH IT, (3) LOOK FOR WAYS IN YOUR LIFE THAT NEED TO BE CHANGED TO ALLOW YOU TO BE MORE CHRISTLIKE.

MONDAY

Pray:

☐ PRAY
☐ READ
☐ RESPOND

Read Luke 4:1-13.

How does Satan most often come to tempt you?

Read Luke 4:1-13 again.

What Scripture verse has been most helpful to you in defeating Satan?

Commitment Prayer:

985003

(1) SPEND TIME FIRST THING IN THE MORNING IF AT ALL POSSIBLE, (2) PRAY BEFORE YOU READ THE PASSAGE ASKING GOD TO SPEAK TO YOU THROUGH IT, (3) LOOK FOR WAYS IN YOUR LIFE THAT NEED TO BE CHANGED TO ALLOW YOU TO BE MORE CHRISTLIKE.

TUESDAY

Pray:

☐ PRAY
☐ READ
☐ RESPOND

Read 1 Corinthians 10:13.

What promise does this verse give about temptation?

Read 1 Corinthians 10:13 again.

Why do Christians often fail to escape temptation?

Commitment Prayer:

985003

(1) SPEND TIME FIRST THING IN THE MORNING IF AT ALL POSSIBLE, (2) PRAY BEFORE YOU READ THE PASSAGE ASKING GOD TO SPEAK TO YOU THROUGH IT, (3) LOOK FOR WAYS IN YOUR LIFE THAT NEED TO BE CHANGED TO ALLOW YOU TO BE MORE CHRISTLIKE.

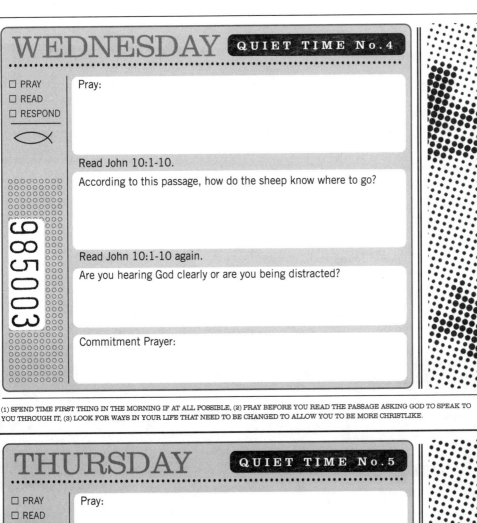

WEDNESDAY

QUIET TIME No. 4

☐ PRAY
☐ READ
☐ RESPOND

985003

Pray:

Read John 10:1-10.

According to this passage, how do the sheep know where to go?

Read John 10:1-10 again.

Are you hearing God clearly or are you being distracted?

Commitment Prayer:

(1) SPEND TIME FIRST THING IN THE MORNING IF AT ALL POSSIBLE, (2) PRAY BEFORE YOU READ THE PASSAGE ASKING GOD TO SPEAK TO YOU THROUGH IT, (3) LOOK FOR WAYS IN YOUR LIFE THAT NEED TO BE CHANGED TO ALLOW YOU TO BE MORE CHRISTLIKE.

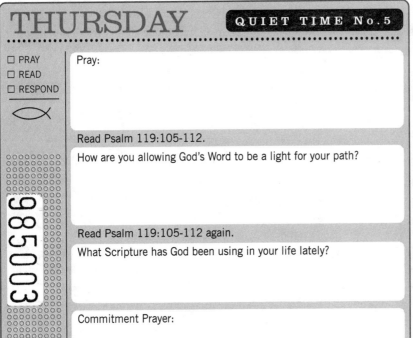

THURSDAY

QUIET TIME No. 5

☐ PRAY
☐ READ
☐ RESPOND

985003

Pray:

Read Psalm 119:105-112.

How are you allowing God's Word to be a light for your path?

Read Psalm 119:105-112 again.

What Scripture has God been using in your life lately?

Commitment Prayer:

(1) SPEND TIME FIRST THING IN THE MORNING IF AT ALL POSSIBLE, (2) PRAY BEFORE YOU READ THE PASSAGE ASKING GOD TO SPEAK TO YOU THROUGH IT, (3) LOOK FOR WAYS IN YOUR LIFE THAT NEED TO BE CHANGED TO ALLOW YOU TO BE MORE CHRISTLIKE.

FRIDAY

Pray:

☐ PRAY
☐ READ
☐ RESPOND

Read 2 Chronicles 7:14.

What is necessary for us to do for God to bring healing to our land?

985003

Read 2 Chronicles 7:14 again.

Why focus on what God's people (instead of the ungodly) should do?

Commitment Prayer:

(1) SPEND TIME FIRST THING IN THE MORNING IF AT ALL POSSIBLE, (2) PRAY BEFORE YOU READ THE PASSAGE ASKING GOD TO SPEAK TO YOU THROUGH IT, (3) LOOK FOR WAYS IN YOUR LIFE THAT NEED TO BE CHANGED TO ALLOW YOU TO BE MORE CHRISTLIKE.

SATURDAY

Pray:

☐ PRAY
☐ READ
☐ RESPOND

Read Luke 6:46-49.

What kind of foundation is your life built on?

985003

Read Luke 6:46-49 again.

What evidence is there that shows your life is built on God?

Commitment Prayer:

(1) SPEND TIME FIRST THING IN THE MORNING IF AT ALL POSSIBLE, (2) PRAY BEFORE YOU READ THE PASSAGE ASKING GOD TO SPEAK TO YOU THROUGH IT, (3) LOOK FOR WAYS IN YOUR LIFE THAT NEED TO BE CHANGED TO ALLOW YOU TO BE MORE CHRISTLIKE.

MEMORY VERSE FOR THE WEEK

EPHESIANS 6:12

Remember that Scripture is your sword. It is your weapon to defend yourself against the attacks of Satan. As you work on memorizing your verse this week, picture yourself sharpening your sword.

God-sized Challenge

1. Often Satan attacks Christians through subtle ways. This week, evaluate the music you listen to. Meet together and bring the your favorite music. As you listen to the songs together, write down the lyrics. Reflect and share with your partner the message that the songwriters and singers are sending you through their lyrics. If you discover any music that Satan is using to bring you down spiritually, get rid of it (recording, CD, or cassette).

2. On the night before His death, Jesus prayed all night. He asked His disciples to pray with Him, but they kept falling asleep. He said that prayer was an important way to avoid falling into temptation. Try it out this week. Meet together in a quiet place. Spend one hour in complete silence praying about temptations that may come against you this week and listening for God to speak to you. After the hour is up, talk about the experience. Share anything specific that God showed you during the time. Write down things you want to remember about this prayer time.

3. Television is another way that Satan's messages enter our minds without us knowing about it. Evaluate what you watch this week. Discuss your favorite television shows. Pick one show that you both watch and agree to watch it together this week. While watching the show, list the different messages the show is giving. Pay attention to subtle suggestions the show makes about the value of people, the holiness of marriage, the place of sexual experience in life, any attitude or reference to God, and the appropriate attitude about self. Discuss the items on your lists after the show. Talk about a criteria you could use for determining which shows you will watch and which you will avoid. (You may prefer to do this challenge with a movie.)

Week-At-A-Glance

Priorities

Essentials

Sunday

MORNING	AFTERNOON	EVENING

Monday

MORNING	AFTERNOON	EVENING

Tuesday

MORNING	AFTERNOON	EVENING

Wednesday

MORNING	AFTERNOON	EVENING

Thursday

MORNING	AFTERNOON	EVENING

Friday

MORNING	AFTERNOON	EVENING

Saturday

MORNING	AFTERNOON	EVENING

Suppose you are on a shuttle craft heading into space. Your rockets are at full speed. Suddenly a giant alien ship blasts away at you with its lasers. If you don't find someone to help, you will be space debris in a matter of seconds. You feel a huge blast hit your shuttle. Someone yells, "The ship is losing integrity!" Oh, no! This is the end.

Why would it be so bad for your shuttle to lose integrity? If you said because that would mean you had a hole in your spaceship, you are right. Integrity is wholeness. It means that everything is whole, just as it should be.

Think about your Christian life as a shuttle craft and the alien ship as Satan and sin. If your Christian life is whole, all of the pieces fit together and there is not a hole blasted out by sin. On the other hand, if there are things in your life that don't look like Christ, your life doesn't have integrity. Warning! Warning!

Sound a bit far-fetched? I'm exaggerating about the shuttle craft to illustrate a point, but this session focuses on a life of wholeness, of integrity, in Christ.

What is Character?
Write your definition of character below.

Everyone has some kind of character. *Character* is a set of traits that defines who you are. Think about one of your best friends. What is characteristic of this person's life? Is your friend honest? Is your friend genuine? Is he or she warm and caring, or does your friend tend to laugh off the problems of others?

Describe one of your best friends.

PSALM 26:1-7

When we know someone well, we start to trust their character. Many teenagers say that their friends have to be people they can trust. They wouldn't consider someone as a friend if he or she was untrustworthy. It is important to have reliable character.

Check out the three situations below. Circle words or phrases that indicate the kind of character the person in the story has.

SITUATION 1
Deion could best be described as a modern-day example of Eddie Haskell on the old "Leave It to Beaver" show. When his parents are around—or the parents of any of his friends—he is kind, humble, and displays excellent manners. But when the adults are not around and it's just Deion and his friends, he is prideful, hateful, and cocky.

SITUATION 2
Susan is one of the most active teenagers in the youth group. She loves to read the Bible, knows a lot about Scripture, and goes on all the youth trips. When she sings in church, she gets praised for her ability. However, Susan has no self-control when it comes to boys. She doesn't show it to those that see her everyday, but just ask her last two boyfriends. They would say that she pressured them to go further in their relationship than she should have. Her last boyfriend quit coming to the youth group

because she wouldn't stop. He did not want to be a part of a youth group that had leaders like Susan. She appears to be one thing at church but quite another on a date.

SITUATION 3
When Jon is working at his part-time job, no one works harder than he does. His boss even made him "Employee of the Month" because he thought that Jon was an excellent employee who cared about doing the job right. However, if you asked those who knew Jon's work habits best—his coworkers—you would hear a totally different story: that Jon only appears to work hard. When the boss is not around, Jon stops what he is doing and takes it easy until he knows the boss is coming back. Then when the boss returns, he will get very busy again. Jon has never learned about what it means to have a Christlike character.

What do you think about these three people? Are they people of godly character? Why or why not?

MATTHEW 12:30 Think about your own character. Does your character have integrity? Is it whole or are there big holes in your character that don't resemble anything godly? The truth is, most of us have areas of our lives that need work. Still, a Christian should never be satisfied with a life of poor character. This was something Paul emphasized in the letters he wrote.

Read 1 Timothy 4:7-8. What does Paul tell Timothy to train himself to be?

How is training for godliness like physical training?

Carter hits the weight room every day after school. Football season is over and a lot of the guys have slacked off on their training, but Carter wants to be ready for the next season. Each week, he is able to do a few more repetitions. He pushes himself to get just one more rep when he feels like he has no strength left. Carter steadily gets stronger.

Think about being in God's gym. There are no weight benches, but there are difficult circumstances that you must overcome. An example of a difficult circumstance in God's gym could be your sister. She is constantly doing things that make you angry. You know how to yell at her, but what you haven't learned to do is to respond to her with patience and

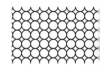

love. So, each day you try a little harder to be patient with her. Each day, you try a little harder to smile instead of scream when she smears your mom's lipstick on your favorite shirt. Little by little, you become a picture of Christ to your sister. You become someone she can look up to.

PROVERBS
4:1-9

Paul was pretty specific about the way that you can develop a godly character. Read these verses in 1 Timothy 4 and answer the questions.

verse 10 - Where did Paul say that we get the power for having a godly character?

verse 12 - Did Paul think it was OK for young people to lack Christian character? ❑ Yes ❑ No If no, what did he think?

verse 13 - To what did Paul tell Timothy to be devoted?

verse 15 - How did Paul tell Timothy to apply himself to these things?

verse 16 - What did Paul tell Timothy would be the result of his perseverance?

Building a godly character does not come from human effort. It is the result of a dependence on God. However, that does not mean that there is no work involved. A Christian has to be devoted fully to God's Word and to right living while seeking God's direction.

ROMANS 8:28

When Paul said that Timothy would save himself and his hearers (v. 16), he did not mean that Timothy would be saved by his good works. Paul was clear that our works cannot save us. (See Eph. 2:8-9.) Rather, Paul was saying that God would work through Timothy to save those who heard Timothy as well as Timothy himself. One of the by-products of a godly character is that your life will be a witness God can use to bring those around you to Himself.

Compare these two stories:
(1) Barry was a Christian, but you wouldn't have known it if you saw him at school. His Christian life had so many holes in it. His language was as bad as anyone's in the school. His relationships with girls were full of compromise and sin. He often felt twinges of guilt and sometimes tried to clean up his act. On one such occasion, he talked to his friend Scott about coming to church with him. Scott laughed. "You go to church?" he asked. "That must not be much of a church."

1 CORINTHIANS
1:18

(2) Connie tried to share with her friend Amber about Christ. Amber was totally disinterested. "Look, Connie," Amber told her. "I know that you are really serious about your religion. It's just not for me." Connie nodded, feeling a little disappointed. "Would you mind if I pray for God to show Himself to you?" Connie asked. Amber looked at her for a long time. Finally, she said, "That would be OK. In fact, that would be kind of cool." Three months later, Amber asked Connie if she could go to church with her. "God means so much to you, He's got to be real," she told Connie.

Think about your character. Are you more like Connie or more like Barry? What changes do you need to make in your character?

Character is not an instant or easy thing to develop. It takes diligence to change sinful habits and behaviors so that they align with Jesus' character.

ECCLESIASTES
3:9-12

I know what you are thinking: *Everyone has character flaws. No one I know has perfect integrity.* If you are looking for human examples of integrity, you are right. No person, other than Jesus, ever totally lived up to the character that God wants us to have. But, all of those imperfect people are not supposed to be the models for our lives. The early church began to be called "Christians" by the non-Christians. The word literally meant "little Christs." They were actually making fun of the believers. Perhaps they said something like, "You all run around trying to be like Jesus. You are a bunch of little Christs." The believers took the name as a badge of honor. The Person Christians try to model their lives after is Jesus.

You could definitely say that Jesus was a man of integrity. He possessed all of the positive character traits we could ever desire. As a matter of fact, Jesus is the definition of integrity. When we want a perfect example of what it is, we have to look no further than Jesus.

Read each of the Scripture passages on the next page. Describe the character that Jesus showed in the way He dealt with the situation.

1. Luke 4:1-13 _____

2. Luke 19:1-10 _____

3. Luke 20:20-26 _____

4. Luke 22:47-53_____

Jesus never cracked in pressure situations. He never let popular opinion keep Him from doing the right thing. His character was whole; He had perfect integrity.

Character is important. The goal of this entire study is to help you be more like Christ, to have His character. That is why a Character Trait Study has been included in each session of this study.

Review the Character Trait Study in each session. In the space after each character trait below, explain how have you tried to develop and apply these character traits during this study.

Responsibility _____
_____

Faithfulness _____
_____

Self-control _____
_____

Joy _____
_____

Patience _____
_____

Humbleness _____
_____

Single-mindedness _____
_____

We will never be perfect as Jesus was, but don't set your sights lower. Strive to be the person of integrity that God has called you to be.

ON YOUR OWN

Read 1 Corinthians 11:1. Paul told the Corinthians to follow his example as he followed the example of Christ. Are you so much a picture of the character of Christ that others could follow you as you follow Christ?

What does Christian character look like? There are many traits that the Bible directs Christians to have. Work through this list, rating yourself on how well your life exhibits each trait. Remember that this is not all of them; there are many more. On a scale of 1 to 10, 1 being the least like you and 10 being most like you, rate yourself on each character trait:

Caring	1	2	3	4	5	6	7	8	9	10
Cheerful	1	2	3	4	5	6	7	8	9	10
Compassionate	1	2	3	4	5	6	7	8	9	10
Confident	1	2	3	4	5	6	7	8	9	10
Cooperative	1	2	3	4	5	6	7	8	9	10
Courageous	1	2	3	4	5	6	7	8	9	10
Courteous	1	2	3	4	5	6	7	8	9	10
Dependable	1	2	3	4	5	6	7	8	9	10
Diligent	1	2	3	4	5	6	7	8	9	10
Fair	1	2	3	4	5	6	7	8	9	10
Forgiving	1	2	3	4	5	6	7	8	9	10
Generous	1	2	3	4	5	6	7	8	9	10
Helpful	1	2	3	4	5	6	7	8	9	10
Honest	1	2	3	4	5	6	7	8	9	10
Joyful	1	2	3	4	5	6	7	8	9	10
Kind	1	2	3	4	5	6	7	8	9	10
Loyal	1	2	3	4	5	6	7	8	9	10
Modest	1	2	3	4	5	6	7	8	9	10
Optimistic	1	2	3	4	5	6	7	8	9	10
Patient	1	2	3	4	5	6	7	8	9	10
Persistent	1	2	3	4	5	6	7	8	9	10
Reliable	1	2	3	4	5	6	7	8	9	10
Respectful	1	2	3	4	5	6	7	8	9	10
Responsible	1	2	3	4	5	6	7	8	9	10
Self-controlled	1	2	3	4	5	6	7	8	9	10
Thoughtful	1	2	3	4	5	6	7	8	9	10
Trustworthy	1	2	3	4	5	6	7	8	9	10

Mark two or three traits that you demonstrate well. You can always improve, even though God has probably already taught you some of these traits.

Choose two or three traits that you need to work on. In the space below, begin to devise a plan for developing those traits to a greater extent in your life. Be sure your plan includes prayer and dependence on God.

CHARACTER TRAIT STUDY

Integrity— A general term used for many Christlike characteristics; it means having the quality of wholeness and honesty. When someone has integrity, it means what they do when people are watch-ing them is the same thing they do when no one is around.

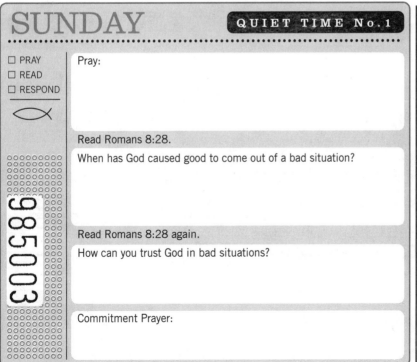

SUNDAY

QUIET TIME No. 1

☐ PRAY
☐ READ
☐ RESPOND

985003

Pray:

Read Romans 8:28.
When has God caused good to come out of a bad situation?

Read Romans 8:28 again.
How can you trust God in bad situations?

Commitment Prayer:

(1) SPEND TIME FIRST THING IN THE MORNING IF AT ALL POSSIBLE, (2) PRAY BEFORE YOU READ THE PASSAGE ASKING GOD TO SPEAK TO YOU THROUGH IT, (3) LOOK FOR WAYS IN YOUR LIFE THAT NEED TO BE CHANGED TO ALLOW YOU TO BE MORE CHRISTLIKE.

MONDAY

Pray:

□ PRAY
□ READ
□ RESPOND

Read Psalm 139:13-16.

What does this verse indicate about how well God knows us?

Read Psalm 139:13-16 again.

How should this affect our attitude toward God?

985003

Commitment Prayer:

TUESDAY

Pray:

□ PRAY
□ READ
□ RESPOND

Read 1 Corinthians 1:18.

What does the cross of Christ mean to you?

Read 1 Corinthians 1:18 again.

Whom do you know who sees the cross as foolishness?

985003

Commitment Prayer:

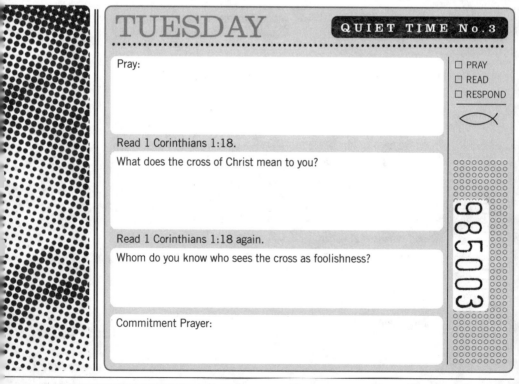

WEDNESDAY

- ☐ PRAY
- ☐ READ
- ☐ RESPOND

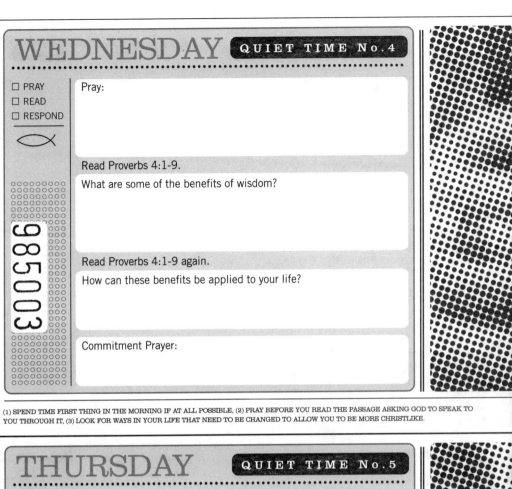

985003

Pray:

Read Proverbs 4:1-9.

What are some of the benefits of wisdom?

Read Proverbs 4:1-9 again.

How can these benefits be applied to your life?

Commitment Prayer:

(1) SPEND TIME FIRST THING IN THE MORNING IF AT ALL POSSIBLE, (2) PRAY BEFORE YOU READ THE PASSAGE ASKING GOD TO SPEAK TO YOU THROUGH IT, (3) LOOK FOR WAYS IN YOUR LIFE THAT NEED TO BE CHANGED TO ALLOW YOU TO BE MORE CHRISTLIKE.

THURSDAY

- ☐ PRAY
- ☐ READ
- ☐ RESPOND

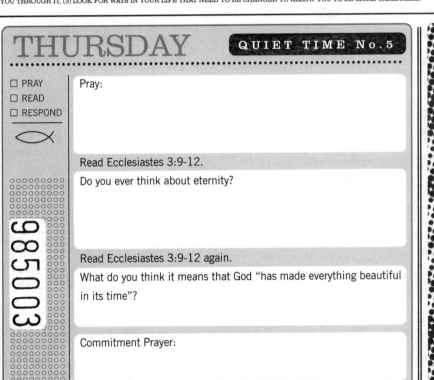

985003

Pray:

Read Ecclesiastes 3:9-12.

Do you ever think about eternity?

Read Ecclesiastes 3:9-12 again.

What do you think it means that God "has made everything beautiful in its time"?

Commitment Prayer:

(1) SPEND TIME FIRST THING IN THE MORNING IF AT ALL POSSIBLE, (2) PRAY BEFORE YOU READ THE PASSAGE ASKING GOD TO SPEAK TO YOU THROUGH IT, (3) LOOK FOR WAYS IN YOUR LIFE THAT NEED TO BE CHANGED TO ALLOW YOU TO BE MORE CHRISTLIKE.

FRIDAY

Pray:

☐ PRAY
☐ READ
☐ RESPOND

Read Psalm 26:1-7.

What words in this passage describe a life of integrity?

Read Psalm 26:1-7 again.

Could your life be described as innocent in the eyes of God?

Commitment Prayer:

985003

SATURDAY

Pray:

☐ PRAY
☐ READ
☐ RESPOND

Read Matthew 12:30.

Do your actions indicate that you are for God or against God?

Read Matthew 12:30 again.

What do you think it means to be a gatherer? A scatterer?

Commitment Prayer:

985003

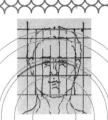

MEMORY VERSES FOR THE WEEK
GALATIANS 5:22-23

Memorizing Scripture is easy to do one verse at a time. Most Christians struggle to memorize Scripture because they see so much that they need to do and try to do it all at once. In this study, you have committed eight passages to memory. That is great, but don't let that be the end. Continue memorizing one verse a week and review those you have already memorized. You will be surprised how quickly your knowledge of Scripture will grow.

God-sized Challenge

This week's God-sized Challenge is to call and invite the guest for whom you have been praying to the Celebration. Before you call, be sure of the time and place of the Celebration. You may need to offer transportation to the person you invite. Look for an opportunity to share your testimony with that individual either before the celebration, during, or after it.

Week-At-A-Glance

Priorities

Essentials

Sunday

MORNING	AFTERNOON	EVENING

Monday

MORNING	AFTERNOON	EVENING

Tuesday

MORNING	AFTERNOON	EVENING

Week-At-A-Glance

Wednesday

MORNING	AFTERNOON	EVENING

Thursday

MORNING	AFTERNOON	EVENING

Friday

MORNING	AFTERNOON	EVENING

Saturday

MORNING	AFTERNOON	EVENING

TOOL BOX
Challenge

How does completing a project make you feel? One of my favorite things is to finish a project, pack up my tools, and move on to something else. Is that how you feel now that you have completed *Basic Student Discipleship*?

So now are you thinking, *OK, now that I've completed this study, I'll pack up my discipleship tools and start something else*? Wait! This is different! Since you are reading this page and you have completed this study, you deserve a pat on the back for a job well done. You have finished the pages of this book, but now you have only the basic tools for discipleship.

Discipleship is about following Jesus throughout your lifetime. Since you have just begun the adventure, you can't quit now! Using this study, you have packed your "discipleship toolbox" with necessary and useful tools. These tools will become more important to your Christian life in the months, even years, to come. Some items in your toolbox include:

- Knowledge that looking and acting like Jesus will cost you something.
- Knowledge that changing your life comes about as a result of your relationship with Jesus.
- Friends to encourage you and hold your accountable.
- Understanding of the importance of putting God first as you plan and prioritize your time.
- Understanding of the importance of Scripture in your knowledge of Jesus and His will for you.
- Knowledge that different types of prayer help you and those for whom you pray.
- Ability to use your Christian ministry to help others and make an eternal investment.
- Knowledge of how to write and share your testimony.
- Realization that you are in a battle and knowledge of how to identify Satan's subtle attacks.
- Ability to identify and develop character traits to help you become more like Jesus.

Wow! That's a lot of tools! Now it's time to use the basic discipleship tools you have gained in this study. Here's your challenge: go beyond the basic! Do you feel like you need more help in your prayer life? Ask your leader to begin an in-depth study on prayer. Do you have a heart to tell others about Jesus, but you want to know more of the Bible so you can better answer their questions? Ask your leader to start a study on the Bible. The more you use your discipleship tools and the more you learn about the tools, the more you will be like Jesus.

Glossary

- **Accept Christ**—To respond to Jesus by deciding to have faith in Him for salvation.
- **Accountability**—Answerable to others, able to explain and take personal responsibility for an action.
- **Apostle**—One sent on a mission. Select witnesses of Jesus called to proclaim His message of salvation.
- **Atonement**—To cover, to cancel one's sins. God in Christ atoned for our sins by dying on the cross.
- **Baptism**—Immersion, submersion. Baptism doesn't save a person but is a symbol of salvation and a sign of obedience to Christ. Water baptism is a picture of death, burial, and resurrection.
- **Believe**—Trust, have confidence in, have faith in, make a commitment to.
- **The Body of Christ**—The church, individual members join to function in unity. Jesus is the head of the body.
- **Born Again**—Christians are often referred to as people who have been born again, a spiritual birth into the family of God.
- **Christ**—Anointed One. One specially chosen for an important purpose. Christ identifies Jesus as God's Messiah, the Savior.
- **Christian**—One committed to Christ and to becoming like Him.
- **Church**—People, a body of believers that have been called out of the world, and that is under the power and authority of Jesus Christ.
- **Confess, Confession**—Openly admit wrongdoing to God and each other.
- **Convicted of sin**—Firm feeling that God wants one to choose or stop an action.
- **Communion**—A term used by some for the Lord's Supper. It is intended to be communion between the believer and the Lord.
- **Converted**—To turn from sin to God, turn about, to turn from wrong actions and attitudes to right ones.
- **Disciple**—Learner, student, follower, apprentice. One who accepts the teacher's teachings and imitates his practices.
- **Discipleship**—Commitment to Christ that includes learning and applying the Bible to life, sharing Christ with others, serving the church, fulfilling the goals God designs for each person.
- **Faith**—Belief, trust. Faith in Jesus Christ is essential for salvation. Faith is active, showing in action and attitude.
- **Forgive, Forgiveness**—Pardon and removal of a wrong. Give up revenge and resentment. Jesus forgave sins when people repented.
- **Gentile**—Literally, *nation*. It refers to a person who is not a Jew.
- **Glorification**—Final condition of being pure or holy—set apart. Only believers are glorified. Takes place at time of death or upon Jesus' second coming.
- **God**—The Eternal One—without beginning and without end. The uncreated One who created everything and everyone. He is One; yet, He reveals Himself to us as three in One: God the Father, God the Son, and God the Holy Spirit. The way to come to know God the Father and God the Spirit is to come to know God the Son, who is Jesus Christ. God is all-powerful, all-knowing, all-present, all-loving.
- **Gospel**—Good news. Message about the life and sacrificial death of Jesus Christ.
- **Grace**—Undeserved favor, Gift of God that provides eternal life for all who trust Jesus Christ as Lord and Savior.
- **Hell**—Place and condition of eternal punishment for those who reject Jesus as Lord and Savior.
- **Holy**—Persons, places, or things set apart for use by God. All holiness originates with God; all Christians are holy and called to live a holy life.
- **Holy Spirit**—God's Spirit and third Person of the Trinity. Lives within all Christians to help them, communicate God's truth to them, convict them of sin, convince them God's ways are right, and comfort them when they are sad.
- **Incarnation**—Literally, *in flesh*. Christ became human and took an earthly body but still kept His divine, sinless nature.
- **Intercession**—Praying or pleading on someone else's behalf.

Character

Guide

Ministry

Prayer

Scripture

Priorities

Accountability

- **Jesus**—Savior. Jesus is the Son of God; He is God the Son. He always was, is, and will be. He existed and was active with the Father in creation. His earthly ministry began when He was about 30 years old and lasted for three years. In obedience to God the Father, Jesus lived a sinless life, suffered an agonizing death on the cross, and provided salvation for all people. God raised Jesus from death to reign with Him forever.
- **Justification**—God's act of declaring and making the repentant sinner right with Him.
- **Kingdom of God**—The rule of God; knowing, loving, and obeying God.
- **The Last Supper**—The actual meal that Jesus shared with His disciples on the eve of His death.
- **The Lord's Supper**—A memorial observance to recall Christ's death, the salvation He brings, and anticipation of His return.
- **Lust**—Desire that turns bad when a person wants something other than what God wants. Lust is a sin of attitude that becomes more serious if it leads to action.
- **Mercy**—Compassion, love, sympathy, deep caring, forgiveness.
- **Messiah**—Literally, *Anointed One*. Savior.
- **Parable**—An earthly story that has a heavenly meaning. It is an everyday truth that has a spiritual application.
- **Pentecost**—The day the Holy Spirit came to Christians after Jesus' resurrection.
- **Pharisee**—Influential group of Jews whose name means *separated ones*.
- **Redemption**—Jesus made a deliberate sacrifice of Himself, providing our redemption from sin and allowing us fellowship with God.
- **Repentance**—The whole process of change that begins with an inward, conscious decision to turn from sin to God.
- **Reconciliation**—Restored relationship. Christ's death provided for the removal of the barrier of sin to bring people back into a right relationship with God.
- **Redeem**—To buy back; to free or pay a price for. Christ's death paid for our sins and frees us from the bondage of sin upon our acceptance of Him. He is our Redeemer.
- **Redemption**—Release that occurs when a price is paid. Jesus paid the price for our release from sin.
- **Repentance**—A turning of the mind, heart, and life through trust in Christ. May simply mean regret or change of mind.
- **Resurrection**—God's raising of the dead in Christ to eternal life. God raised Jesus from death.
- **Revelation**—Uncovering, revealing that which is hidden.
- **Righteous**—Right with God. A person is made right only through God in Christ.
- **Salvation**—The experience of being converted from being a person without Christ to a person with Christ as Savior and Lord, and being delivered from the consequences of being separated from God through sin.
- **Sanctification**—The growing of the Christian into a lifestyle of honoring and serving God.
- **Saved**—Describes the present condition of a believer who has trusted Jesus Christ for salvation through faith.
- **Spiritual Gifts**—Abilities that God gives through the Holy Spirit to all Christians to equip them to perform His service.
- **Sanctify**—Set apart. Dedicate as holy and for God's use. All Christians are sanctified.
- **Satan**—The devil. The evil one. The enemy. Adversary. Satan directly opposes God.
- **Savior**—Deliverer; one who saves.
- **Sin**—Action or attitude that disobeys God, betrays Him, or fails to do good.
- **Spirit**—Usually means the Holy Spirit. The Holy Spirit is the third Person of the Trinity. He enables the believer to grow in Christ and please the Father.
- **Spiritual Gifts**—Abilities given to believers by the Holy Spirit.
- **Steward, Stewardship**—Accountability for deciding best ways to spend the time, talents, money, and possessions God has given to us.
- **Temple**—House or place of worship. Temple can also refer to a Christian or a group of believers.
- **Temptation**—Enticement to do wrong. Comes from Satan and is deceptive. Temptation is not sin, but yielding to it is.

Definitions adapted from *Student Daymaker* (Nashville: LifeWay Press, 1996).

Character

Guide

Ministry

Prayer

Scripture

Priorities

Accountability

Cost

Write your testimony by answering the three questions on this worksheet. After you have answered the questions, read and edit your responses. Don't glorify your sinful life, but pay more attention to how you became a Christian and what your life is like as a Christian. After you have edited your testimony, practice reading it aloud. Practice saying it to your accountability partner, leader, or family member. Use this sheet as a handy reference whenever you are called on to give your testimony.

What was your life like before you accepted Jesus as your Savior and Lord?

What actually happened when you accepted Jesus as your Savior and Lord?

What has your life been like since you accepted Jesus as your Savior?

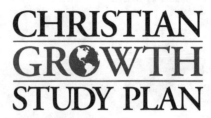

CHRISTIAN GROWTH STUDY PLAN

In the **Christian Growth Study Plan (formerly Church Study Course),** this book *Basic Student Discipleship* is a resource for course credit in the subject area Personal Life of the Christian Growth category of plans. To receive credit, read the book, complete the learning activities, show your work to your pastor, a staff member or church leader, then complete the following information. This page may be duplica-ted. Send the completed page to:

Christian Growth Study Plan, One LifeWay Plaza, Nashville, TN 37234-0117
FAX: (615)251-5067 E-mail: cgspnet@lifeway.com

For information about the Christian Growth Study Plan, refer to the Christian Growth Study Plan Catalog. It is located online at *www.lifeway.com/cgsp*. If you do not have access to the Internet, contact the Christian Growth Study Plan office, (1.800.968.5519) for the specific plan you need for your ministry.

Basic Student Discipleship CG-0804

PARTICIPANT INFORMATION

Social Security Number (USA ONLY-optional)	Personal CGSP Number*	Date of Birth (MONTH, DAY, YEAR)
Name (First, Middle, Last)		Home Phone
Address (Street, Route, or P.O. Box)	City, State, or Province	Zip/Postal Code

CHURCH INFORMATION

Church Name		
Address (Street, Route, or P.O. Box)	City, State, or Province	Zip/Postal Code

CHANGE REQUEST ONLY

☐ Former Name		
☐ Former Address	City, State, or Province	Zip/Postal Code
☐ Former Church	City, State, or Province	Zip/Postal Code
Signature of Pastor, Conference Leader, or Other Church Leader		Date

*New participants are requested but not required to give SS# and date of birth. Existing participants, please give CGSP# when using SS# for the first time. Thereafter, only one ID# is required. **Mail to:** Christian Growth Study Plan, One LifeWay Plaza, Nashville, TN 37234-0117. Fax: (615)251-5067.

Rev. 10-01